D0984746

House Calls

Modern-day Tales of Wonder and Woe
from an Ancient Profession

C. GRESHAM BAYNE, M.D.
The Godfather of Home-care Medicine

A personal memoir

JOHN FREEMAN, EDITOR

Front cover:
Science and Charity
oil painting by Pablo Picasso in 1897 at age 15

A young Picasso provides insight into late 19th century medicine in Spain. We see a patient lying ill in a room, eyes closed, on a bed. A nun is at the bedside delivering tea or medicine, holding a child, presumably that of the patient.

On the opposite side of the bed, we see the stern-faced physician (Picasso's father served as the model), as he takes the patient's pulse by holding her right wrist and looking at his pocket watch.

—————————————

Photo by John Freeman, October 2018,
during a visit to Musée Picasso, Paris,
where painting was on temporary loan
from Museu Picasso in Barcelona, Spain.

To Deirdre, for all the missed obligations,
late dinners, promises reneged,
and most of all for raising our two wonderful children.
You are the wind beneath my wings.

CONTENTS

Author's Introduction

As I WRITE THIS, the world finds itself mired in a pandemic caused by the COVID-19 coronavirus. So far, the virus has proven to be highly contagious, difficult to detect and too-often lethal.

Our nation, along with nearly all 50 states, has issued a series of strict orders, urging all of us to stay home to combat the virus by social distancing from each other for weeks, months or perhaps longer.

Meanwhile, the dance of life and, ultimately, death continues.

When we get too sick from cancer, heart disease, diabetes, etc., we have to go to the hospital, where all the most critical COVID-19 patients are now struggling to stay alive. Of course, that's the last place you want to go (or should go) if you don't need to go.

Yet, with the now-advanced evolution of physicians' house calls to treat the urgently ill, a growing trend so obvious to me and 3,000 other mobile doctors, you still don't hear much about the benefits of such highly personalized, in-home care.

Why?

You're about to find out.

———✺———

My house-call patients were typically over 80 years old, predominantly female because males tend to be dead by that time, with physical infirmities that make office visits a struggle if not impossible.

Over half were suffering from some form of dementia. A fourth of house call patients die annually, a higher mortality rate than oncologists typically experience.

With healthcare remaining the most common cause of bankruptcy in the United States, the majority of homebound patients are also poor and qualify for Medicaid, making mobile medicine inherently an affirmative action program.

Here, you will learn about such remarkable patients as Faith Klevens, perhaps the first person to have her life saved in real time by telemonitoring data transmitted to her doctor flying on a commercial airplane.

And you'll meet The Man Who Wouldn't Die, a glorious WWII submarine hero who suffered an inglorious death with courage.

Then there's Benjie, the Hairless Chihuahua.

———✧✧✧———

Looking back, I consider my greatest privilege has been that of re-introducing the advantages of house call medicine to modern society. That is the purpose of this book.

Here, you will see how Air Force One was altered to carry our house call equipment after President Bush was transported unnecessarily by helicopter to the hospital, leaving a man who couldn't spell "potato" to run the country.

You will see why bringing medical care into dirt floor homes of the poor and disadvantaged makes sense, and why famous figures like Dr. Benjamin Spock, Jerry Lewis, and boxing champ Oscar de la Hoya asked me to be their doctor after their first house call, and freely gave permission to use their stories.

Through the years, my house call practice was widely featured by *Medical Marvels*, the *Today Show* (twice), the *New York Times*, *L.A. Times*, *Wall Street Journal*, *Modern Maturity*, and *Reader's Digest*, by full-page articles in *Time, People*, and *Forbes Magazines*, as well as numerous evergreen news reports across the country.

Here, you will peek inside the white coat of medicine and learn why change is so hard for our profession, and how disruption by the insurance industry's incredible financial power over Congress can be disrupted only by community-based physicians making house calls.

This is also a book about some surprising good news in healthcare, told through my patients' own stories and through a large federal study based in large part upon the principles I helped develop for mobile physicians over the past 40 years.

—⁓⁓—

Virtually ever since I started making house calls, my colleagues, friends and patients have been constantly telling me: "You *have* to write these stories."

The effort of documentation began through my daily notes begun in 1987, so I am reasonably confident of the accuracy of the tales. Obviously, some patient's names have been changed where appropriate to protect their privacy.

What began formally over three years ago as "Call Doctor," the professional memoir of my life as a physician-entrepreneur, initially took the form of a business-themed narrative of how I raised and spent $30 million from a handful of the most savvy investors in the country through nine financing rounds or "restarts."

Losing money each of the first 17 years, we reached profitability only on the eve of the early 2000s dot-com disaster, which made the story uneventful to most, and unprofitable to all concerned.

A second literary effort devolved into a technical treatise of how we managed to merge all the diagnostic tools of emergency medicine into a house call practice, leaving the reader likely bored, yet wondering why they had never heard of 1-800-CALL DOC, a national platform for house call physicians in 11 cities in five states by 1996.

It's in this third effort that I believe full value was sought and found, the story of how my pursuit of a dream for all the right reasons eventually led to a national movement in homecare medicine that truly has the potential for saving American healthcare.

If I dare be so immodest.

During that bumpy journey, I learned how pride was a weak surrogate for compassion; how the focus on doing what is right for the patient can overcome virtually any barrier placed in the way by conventional medicine practices; and most importantly, how caring about others can heal your soul.

Of the hundreds of men and women who helped Call Doctor along its way, the list begins with my sister Carol, and her incredibly generous husband, Ted Price, who funded our first efforts and taught me the basics of entrepreneurship.

It culminates with Dr. Patrick Soon-Shiong, in my view the world's greatest living physician, who salvaged our JanusOS electronic medical records company and continues to believe in the potential for comprehensive care distributed through patient's homes.

When they write the story about who cured cancer, it will undoubtedly conclude with Dr. Soon-Shiong.

Along the way, investors such Bill Grant, Martin Fenton, Barbara Freeman, and Jim Berglund deserve my eternal gratitude for their leadership and resilient ability to restart a company which had a frustrating habit of going bankrupt.

If there ever was a model to prove capitalism can be a foundation for new ideas that benefit the unfortunate, it is their continued support for Call Doctor which proved it true.

Few physician/entrepreneurs are fortunate enough to find a CEO who can tolerate our often-overbearing medical personalities. With the better part of a decade's leadership from Jim Collins, I was blessed with a partner both respected by the business community and admired by all those who know him.

One can never repay one's family for all the torment and lost hours stolen by a beeper than stayed on 24/7 for more than 30 years. How my two children grew up so successfully is solely attributed to their mother's relentless ability to "do the right thing."

I can never repay her, although I will continue to try.

C. Gresham Bayne, M.D.
May 2020

A CAREER OF FIRSTS

C. Gresham Bayne, MD

1978:
- First article published documenting vascular bubbles in asymptomatic divers
- First U.S. physician to perform a free ascent from 300FSW in the open sea

1978:
- First to publish a large series of decompression sickness victims (50) treated with no sequelae (no previous disease or injury)
- First book (co-authored) on comprehensive physician training in diving medicine

1979:
- First to measure cardiac output during flight in a helicopter
- First residency-trained emergency physician in the Navy, San Diego
- First Chairman of the first Department of Emergency Medicine in the U.S. Navy

1980:
- First PA catheter floated in the emergency room on a heat stroke victim proving RV failure
- First (and only) published article condemning use the McSwain Dart
- First documentation of higher cardiac output with open chest massage

1981:
- First to prove cerebral air embolism in a free swimmer

1982:
- First to open three chests in the ER at one time
- First to start ER residency program in the U.S. Navy and California

1985:
- First to use oxygen to prevent decompression sickness in tunnel workers
- First lab on a house call
- First needle cricothyreotomy with HFPV producing normal ABGs in the field
- First to do 32 cricothyreotomies in the field during civilian treatments
- First to measure cardiac output during flight
- First above-the-knee amputation in the field with LifeFlight

1986:
- First EKG done on a house call

1987:
- First portable X ray on house calls

1991:
- First use of oximetry as standard on house calls

1995:
- First to measure cardiac output on a house call
- First cardiac impedance sent wirelessly

1999:
- First use of paperless, wireless EMR on HC

2006:
- First BMP and troponin on HC

2007:
- First portable digital x rays on HC
- First Bluetooth CO Starling Curve sent from home
- First paperless, wireless, phoneless and keyboard-less medical practice in U.S.

PART 1

Getting Started

CHAPTER 1

I broke down in tears

"A good surgeon never gets emotionally involved with their patients."

IT WAS OBVIOUS THAT MY PATIENT WAS GOING TO DIE. For me, the futility of our efforts in saving the life of this patriot, who would soon be leaving his three small children fatherless, was excruciating.

I was becoming emotionally unsteady. No wonder. I hadn't slept in nine nights – or days.

Yet, the customary "standard of care" required me to take him back one more time to the operating room for yet another failed, painful procedure. I had been in the same clothes so long that boils were breaking out on my backside.

Worse than boils on my butt, I had reached the breaking point. I was physically, mentally and spiritually exhausted.

Reduced to a trance-like state, no longer in control of what few conscious and coherent thought patterns I had been able to muster only minutes before, I wandered off to the doctor's lounge just off the intensive care unit.

There, in what I thought was my temporary sanctuary, I broke down in tears, crying like I had never cried before.

Eventually, my sobbing subsided, but I was shaken by the wholly unexpected, thoroughly involuntary nature of my emotional response. I was doing my job, seeing patients, responsibly caring for them with the highest level of care I knew.

Perhaps I cared too much.

Because I knew full well that as doctors we weren't supposed to "get emotionally involved," and crying on the job probably wasn't something that gets you elected to national medical societies.

As it turned out, an overly officious nurse told my chief resident that I had been shedding tears.

Hearing that, the chief resident immediately took over the surgery himself and ordered me to go home. I have never heard of this happening before or since – a surgeon-in-training being relieved of his duties due to sheer and utter exhaustion. Thank God for my chief resident, Dr. Ed Aucoin. He did the right thing.

I hadn't. And I knew it.

The next day, I was called in to the Chief of Surgery's office for what might be described as a "disciplinary hearing," the only one I've ever had as a doctor.

No mention was made of the devotion to duty shown by nine consecutive days and nights living and breathing within ten yards of the patient's bedside. No criticism was offered on the operations and surgical management of the patient.

The only advice I was given was something like "a good surgeon never gets emotionally involved with their patients."

———

By 1985, I had already used much of my life's savings to construct the first Mobile Physician Treatment Center, which then lay plugged in to the house while parked in my driveway. It was quite prominent with its large red letters stating "Members, Scripps Memorial Medical Staff."

An executive at Scripps privately told me that the name "Scripps" was highly protected for obvious reasons, but they couldn't stop a statement of truth. All six of the founding doctors at Call Doc were, in fact, members of the Scripps Memorial Hospital medical staff.

Why was it that patients still needed to have a building behind the trust they might place in their physician?

Once we had received our initial million-dollar funding from Galen Partners investment group in 1989, we tested a series of focus groups, largely because I was adamant that the doctor-patient relationship should not be built on a building's reputation, but rather on the strength and trust of a physician willing to come to your home.

The catch phrase I was sure the blinded-patient focus groups would pick for our service would be something like, "When you're sick, there is no place like home."

In fact, they hated that one.

"We old people don't like the word 'sick' when we think about healthcare," said one lady. Such is the complexity of starting a new medical delivery system. I had much to learn about human behavior.

UC San Diego hired a consulting firm before LifeFlight first arrived, spending two years and gobs of money finding out the real problem we faced was a physician backlash.

Regional doctors resented the idea of a helicopter that could fly into their practice area and whisk their patient away to a distant trauma center, even one with clearly better abilities to treat major injuries.

I was not smart enough to research physician backlash for our new house call service, and paid the price in diverse ways.

It only took one air helicopter crash with a doctor on board to remove all physicians from routine placement in pre-hospital air medical transports. Only in the military does this now occur routinely.

With five paramedics killed in ambulance transports annually, one wonders why the paramedic union hasn't done something about their own risks, but I suspect life insurance and other options for paramedics are much less than for physicians.

By 2001, my philosophical transition into a mobile physician was complete. It took only 100 to 120 total patients to constitute a full-time house call practice, given the instability of the homebound elderly.

I fell in love with all of them.

CHAPTER 2

A different drummer

"The middle colic should be hiding somewhere around here."

I WAS BORN TO BE A SURGEON, just not a very good one.

That terrifying thought again paid me an unwelcome visit when I was doing my first hemicolectomy, that is, surgical removal of half of the large bowel.

In many patients, this is a potentially curable procedure, and mine was a reasonably good candidate. At age 40, he was young to have the disease, but with no other health problems he should do well and live a normal lifespan, shortened only by his maleness.

In those days (1975), we had no fancy staplers, gadgets or gizmos to make the operation go fast or even faster. The surgery required you to place two clamps across an inch or so of the fatty tissue surrounding the colon, cut between them with a fancy pair of scissors called "Metzenbaums," then tie off the two fatty sides and move on, one inch at a time.

Every surgeon knows that lurking furtively in the fatty tissue about halfway around the colon is the strategic middle colic artery, pumping its life-sustaining blood supply to the entire small bowel and half of the large colon.

In 1975 and forever before, if you happened to inadvertently snip that artery, even in the slightest, the patient was dead.

Clamp…cut…tie.

Clamp…cut…tie.

Clamp…cut…tie.

With the patient's belly wide open, on and on we went, slowly making our way around the inner circumference of the large bowel, a methodical process that lulled me into a sense of complacency.

Suddenly, to my horror, I realized I had squeezed my "Metz" scissors only to find my cut was blocked by the staff surgeon's stainless-steel clamp.

Here I was, training in the premier military hospital in the world, and my mentor, Dr. Richard Virgilio, who had a hand's-on philosophy, believing that "man learns best by traumatic experience," had just saved me – and my patient's life – from making a fatal mistake.

Dr. Virgilio had been pulled at the end of his first year of surgical internship back in 1965 to go to China Beach, the surgical unit near Da Nang during the height of the Vietnam War. He was now inculcating our surgery teams with his invaluable experience.

Slowly, the staff surgeon teased apart the fatty tissue between the sharp edges of my scissors. Softly, he told me: "The middle colic should be hiding somewhere around here."

And there it was – only an instant from being transected by scissors controlled only by my impulsive, ADHD-addled brain. I had become completely bored with the operation, with the whole idea of surgery for that matter. I mean, for goodness sake, isn't the gallbladder always located in the right upper quadrant?

At that time, I was in the middle of my third year of surgical training – and that was the day I knew I had to quit.

Because of the incredible volume of cases we did at the Navy Hospital, San Diego, I already completed the 600 "major cases" needed to sit for my boards in general surgery, but you couldn't take the boards without completing all five years of training.

I was numb thinking my future life would be measured in "hernia-equivalents," or a number representing the complexity of operations you did last week in terms of hernia repairs.

I needed to talk to patients who were not anesthetized, who could give me their entire medical and social history, who could engage my soul in helping them get well. I needed to think of patients as unique individuals, rather than "the hemicolectomy in room 216."

My fellow surgery residents had been right when they repeatedly told me: "You answer to the call of a different drummer." It was not intended as a compliment.

That "different drummer" was something very different from the adage of many surgeons: "A chance to cut is a chance to cure."

That "drummer" was something different, something that could hold my interest, something that didn't rely on being fast with technique but more likely on being a good listener.

Someone like Dr. Francis Weld Peabody, the revered Harvard Medical School professor of the early 1900s, who famously said: "The secret in caring for patients is to care for the patient."

—◦◦◦—

My first operation as a surgical resident didn't go so well. Perhaps it was a metaphor for the next half-century of my medical practice, as things were never as they appeared in the hospital setting.

The patient was an 18-year-old Navy recruit who was scheduled to go to sea on a nuclear missile submarine during the end of the Cold War. He had a congenital hernia, a little sac that slips down the inguinal canal in some men and can get trapped, creating a surgical emergency.

In those days, when we found an inguinal hernia in a submariner, we fixed it, thinking the nation's security was more important than the minimal risks of minor surgery. After all, surfacing a ballistic missile submarine simply to off-load a medical emergency would let the Russians know where it was, so preventive hernia repairs were done routinely.

I was learning the art of medicine quickly, having spent only three years in medical school.

"My patient," as we tended to call people in those paternalistic days of the past, was asleep under general anesthesia being administered by an oral surgeon who was learning basic anesthesia techniques for the first time.

By some cruel quirk of fate, the same thing held true for me.

I was learning for the first time how to hold a #10 blade scapel and cut into human flesh. Smart people avoid elective surgeries after July 1, when everyone begins their training cycle anew.

My first incision was about a micrometer deep and produced no bleeding. My proctor, the Chief Surgical Resident at Balboa Naval Hospital in San Diego, was impatient and said something like, "Cut like you mean it. We don't have all day!"

As I gingerly advanced the incision inches from the patient's manhood anatomy, I noticed there really wasn't much to it. He didn't bleed. The anatomy looked just like the books I had studied the night before.

Better yet, he was asleep, so the screaming that defined surgical expertise through the Civil War wasn't a problem. I became more confident, even aggressive.

Cutting deeply, I noticed that despite cutting into something that looked a lot like a big vein with dark blue blood oozing slowly from both ends, it was no real problem. I just blotted it with the sponge in my left hand.

Simple enough.

That was about the time all hell broke loose. Dr. Ernie Kundert looked over the green sheets hiding the patient from us at the oral surgery resident, sitting pale on a stool.

"What's going on?" he said loudly.

"I'm having trouble getting a blood pressure," the pale resident said meekly.

Dr. Kundert screamed, "That's because he's dead!" and ripped the sheets from his chest to begin CPR.

I stood motionless with the scalpel in my right hand and just a few spots of blood on my gloved hands, inwardly grateful that the mask over my face disguised me from the nurses in the room.

Since the patient was paralyzed on a ventilator with a tube in his airway and Dr. Kundert was doing chest compressions, there really wasn't much for me to do, except be terrified.

I remembered vaguely something I heard in medical school that "hospitals can be dangerous places," but I really had no idea they were this dangerous.

Luckily for all involved, Dr. Kundert knew what he was doing, so the patient, who had been overdosed on some of the anesthesia drugs, recovered completely and was taken to the Recovery Room after a few stitches in the superficial wound I had created over his hernia.

As the "surgeon," it was my job to tell him what had happened when he woke up, although I really didn't feel I was responsible for any of it.

"Well, young man," I begin hesitantly. "I have some bad news and some good news for you. The bad news is you still have your hernia."

"What's the good news?" he slurred.

"You're alive!" I said proudly, telling him the awful story.

CHAPTER 3

This was big business

"I went back to the bank the next day in great puffery."

EVEN TODAY, IT'S ESTIMATED that more than 100,000 major complications occur every year in American hospitals, killing some 60% of patients with well-meaning attempts at medical care.

Then consider this: According to a 2017 Johns Hopkins study, more than 250,000 people in the U.S. die every year from medical errors. In fact, medical errors are the third-leading cause of death after heart disease and cancer.

Fact is, the first exam I ever did on a real patient hadn't gone well, either. It was the beginning of my third year in medical school, and the patient was an 84-year-old woman in the intensive care unit.

Not knowing about the reflex slowing of the heart from vagal nerve stimulation, I did a rectal exam to be complete. With my gloved finger shoved up where the sun don't shine, the poor lady suddenly arrested.

Her heart simply stopped from the increased vagal tone we get with anal distention. It is the same reason people sometimes faint on the toilet. The heart slows down, so blood flowing to the brain doesn't carry enough oxygen to keep you conscious.

After a chaotic Code Blue, we got her back just like my first surgical patient, and I was initiated into the modern practice of medicine, where everything, including a simple rectal exam, can threaten the life of a patient.

———◦∿∿◦———

My house call practice got started formally in 1987 after several serendipitous relationships and at least one miracle had led to funding with $300,000 from three of the most prestigious investment bankers in America.

They were impressed that we had built a Mobile Physician Treatment Center, providing all the capabilities of the ER in your driveway.

After two years of vetting the concept of urgent house calls to various neighbors and church members, I was convinced this was how we should deliver medicine – on the patient's terms, and in their own homes.

The intensity of the positive reinforcement I received on virtually every house call was amazing. Dozens of patients meeting me for the first time asked if they could invest in "my business."

Of course, taking investment monies from a patient crosses all sorts of boundaries, but I was fortunate to have a supportive sister and her husband, a nationally-known figure in the mysterious (to me) investment banking world.

I remember his frustration after funding the first van, nearly pushing me out the door to "get serious and raise enough money to make it into a business."

I had virtually no idea what he was talking about.

Six months later, I held promises for $50,000 checks from the three national figures with names you might recognize, matched by $25,000 checks from six Scripps doctors who trusted me enough to create what is called a "Reg D" offering of $300,000.

I began thinking about the national fame I would get from solving the Medicare fiscal crisis.

We were scheduled to close this "A-round" financing on October 19, 1987. You might recognize the date as "Black Monday," the day the stock market crashed in the largest single-day drop of the Dow Jones Index in history – as much as 25%.

There was world-wide financial chaos.

I received a call in the late morning from my lead investor in New York saying that despite his promise of $50,000, he could only wire $25,000 that day. He said margin calls created by the market collapse had caused a real problem for one of his close friends who needed bailing out.

Looking back, I'm embarrassed to admit that without any real discussion with my wife and two small kids, I immediately went to the bank and mortgaged my house (again) to cover the $25,000 shortfall.

I had no savings, but this was big business, my big chance to re-form the entire industry of healthcare. I wasn't about to lose the opportunity to take credit for what was clearly going to be such a gigantic success story.

Armed with my handful of large checks and wire-transfers, I went back to the bank the next day in great puffery. I was anticipating the look of surprise and respect that would soon fill the face of the bank official privileged to open my new, *corporate* account.

After going through the minimal formalities required at the time, the moment I was waiting for came. The attractive bank representative said: "Now, how much would you like to open the account with, Dr. Bayne?"

"Three… hundred… thousand … dollars…." I said trying to act like the way an investment banker would act, having no idea what that was. I waited for her stunned look of respect.

"And what color checks would you like us to print for you?" she said, without looking up. Without so much as a clue, I had begun my steep learning curve unpacking the many secrets in the big business of medicine.

———⟡———

One quickly learns while making house calls that the patient's needs become unique in their familial context and are often different than what we assume from the isolated sanctum of our ivoried medical towers.

It is the social context during which a medical event occurs that is often most important to the patient. It can be as simple as the lady suffering a rare and severe asthmatic attack, whose new cat waltzed in the room as I gave her the requisite shots of epinephrine and steroids.

Or as complex as the 96-year-old lady who called me to evaluate her chair-bound husband's cancerous scalp lesion. Upon arrival, I noticed her own scalp was bleeding from a recent fall. Taking a brief history, I found her fall had the historical features of "cardiogenic syncope," leading to her own emergency admission that day. Her husband's lesion could wait.

We forget what we lost by changing the direction of care from the doctor in the home to having patients come to our waiting rooms. With mobile medicine, rather than scheduled office visits, we open up access to anyone with an address.

We lower the barrier to entry for true urgent events that are often missed by the lay public. Most of all, by bringing comprehensive care into the home, we can restore the integrity of the family unit, allowing multi-generational families to care for each other as they age in place.

In our 9-1-1 system, we respond with an ambulance and two paramedics to almost anyone who calls claiming to need aid.

Only recently have we started to integrate such calls with a physician who can triage non-life-threatening emergencies to a less expensive solution…like the doctor's office visit or house call as appropriate. In our most dire moments, 9-1-1 delivers a paramedic to our door usually within ten minutes, but with a less than one-in-five chance that such a rapid response was actually needed.

Physician home visits in a local community have the potential for replacing most of these non-selective ambulance rides with an urgent home visit, just like the physicians routinely did prior to the advent of health insurance in the 1960s.

Instead of transport as the goal, the goal of home visits becomes a safe disposition, which offers the potential for great savings, less of the "lights and sirens" cacophony we are accustomed to, and repatriation to your family physician for the vast majority of symptoms.

In France, it has been standard for decades to place a doctor in every ambulance unit through their "S.A.M.U." system ("*Systeme Ambulance Medecin Urgence.*")

The doctor's role, in addition to emergency care, is to decide if transport is needed or to provide definitive care on scene when possible without transport. Of course, an American paramedic is paid more than physicians in many countries.

With 25% of all hospital admissions coming through the emergency room, and two-thirds of the elderly ambulance patients admitted to the hospital, shifting the dynamic of care into the home has obvious financial repercussions.

In America, the average charge for an ambulance transport is about ten times what a typical physician house call charges even when using lab and portable X-ray.

Yet, the ambulance charge is just for transport to see the same doctor that might have come to see you at home (in my case, in San Diego). When I petitioned the San Diego City Council in 2001 to create an integrated 5-1-1/house call service with emergency physicians doing the triage, it was projected to save the City of San Diego over $21 million annually. Unfortunately, the paramedic union went to battle stations to block any changes.

At the time, San Diego was dispatching an average of 105 ambulances daily through the 9-1-1 Dispatch Centers. Although 80% of them were clearly not for life-threatening conditions, it was still the goose that laid the golden egg.

We have met the enemy, and it is us, for letting such an inefficient system continue virtually unrecognized in its duplicity.

The good news is that now that Medicare has completed a four-year phase-in program of payment denials for ambulance transports when "another form of transportation would not reasonably be expected to harm the patient," the ambulance industry is finally consolidating around the expanded concept of "paramedic house calls."

Hopefully, such programs will be integrated with the primary care physician's oversight, especially when the physician is committed to making mobile visits in follow up to any urgent condition found by paramedics.

Since two-thirds of all ambulance income comes through various federal health insurance programs, only such restrictions to the payment methodology can have any hope of redirecting this expensive transportation industry to one of clinical home visits. Urgent medical care delivered by mobile doctors or paramedics with physician oversight would allow society to shift policy decisions to a more simplistic concept.

First emergency-trained doctors can decide whether initial stabilization and treatment for urgent problems can be done at home (or, as we shall in Chapter 21, a Presidential retreat). Definitive diagnosis and treatment for many conditions (e.g. Grave's Disease treated with beta blockade) can await more complete labs, imaging, or possibly office consultations with specialists like the cardiologist.

This subtle shift in approach makes patients happy and leaves them with more control over the process.

At the same time, it dramatically reduces costs and risks inherent in ambulance runs (about 5 medics or patients die annually during transport collisions).

It also allows policymakers to segregate costs better: We can all agree that Americans deserve access to catastrophic care all the time, but can we really afford to pay for every little healthcare complaint being transported in an ambulance or treated in the emergency room?

CHAPTER 4

Blood, sweat and spit

"I am confident he'll be much better the day after tomorrow."

OSCAR DE LA HOYA DIDN'T LOOK LIKE a prizefighter to me.

He seemed too small and somewhat unsure of himself—wanting his legendary agent Bob Arum, owner of Top Rank Boxing, to make all the decisions for him.

He spoke only Spanish and my Spanish was limited to "two tacos with catsup, por favor."

It was Tuesday, February 1, 1993 and Arum had called me urgently to come see him at the boxer's secret enclave because Oscar had a fever and was supposed to fight in five days.

"This is not complicated," I began, after examining him. "Oscar has a large abscess on the back of his right thigh that is causing the fever of 101.5, an elevated white count over 14,000, and the pain he is experiencing."

I continued: "Normally, he would be admitted to the hospital for a minor operation due to the cellulitis that surrounds the abscess and is invading his bloodstream, but all he really needs is for the abscess to be drained and packed open, and given some antibiotics."

Obviously concerned, Arum replied, "This is his first nationally-televised prizefight. It's on ABC's Wide World of Sports this Saturday. Will he be able to fight Saturday at 1 o'clock?"

"Most likely," I told him. "Typically, people feel worse the next day after we release the pus, since some of it usually invades their bloodstream with the surgery, but I have already given him intravenous antibiotics covering 98% of the bugs we see in these things, and this one looks like a simple staphylococci abscess."

I summed up: "Since he didn't get it in the hospital where the drug-resistant bugs live, I am confident he'll be much better the day after tomorrow."

"OK, cut him," said Arum, definitively.

Shades of the movie *Rocky* flit through my head. I went through the formalities of informed consent with Oscar through a staff member who translated what I said into Spanish.

Then I began the procedure.

I packed his abscess open with sterile gauze, applied a special dressing, gave him a prescription for antibiotics and told his staff to take his temperature every four hours, and to call if it didn't go down by dinnertime.

Oscar was the perfect patient, polite and uncomplaining. I had no idea he would become one of the most famous and successful fighters of our time, winning the World Boxing Championship in four weight categories.

The next day, I received a panicked call from Arum. "Oscar woke up sick today. He feels terrible!"

I asked if he had a fever, and the answer was, "No, but he just feels awful!"

"OK, I'll be right over, but this is probably what I was talking about ... the day-after syndrome and nothing more."

Indeed, it was, and the wound was healing well.

The surrounding cellulitis was all but gone, and both his fever and his white count (an indication of systemic infection) had returned to normal. I reassured Oscar and Arum that he would be much better the next day, and ready to fight Saturday.

Then, Arum dropped his little bombshell: "Doc, I need to be certain he is going to feel well tomorrow. Before 5 pm today, I can cancel the fight without losing my million-dollar guarantee. If I don't notify the ring by 5 pm that he is too sick to fight today, I'm out a million bucks!"

———

From the biopsy of a leper on an island in the Persian Gulf to the rarified offices of New York bankers, through the chairmanship of the world's largest military emergency department, through years moonlighting as a UCSD LifeFlight physician, I had learned some simple skills that saved Oscar de la Hoya's first nationally-televised prize fight.

Bob Arum was so happy that my prediction of Oscar's health had come true the next day, he called to say there were two VIP ring-side tickets for the fight waiting for me on Saturday.

I proudly took my son and sat next to Arum and Oscar's entourage, with plastic mats covering our make-shift tables to protect us from the flying blood, sweat and spit.

I looked to make sure my bandage over Oscar's thigh wound packed with gauze was holding. It was.

In the ring, Oscar looked calm, almost bored.

His opponent was gesticulating and-shadow boxing with fists so fast I couldn't see them. He was an Adonis, sculpted as if Michelangelo himself had carved his muscles. I was worried for Oscar's sake, since he really just looked like a skinny teen-ager to me.

Oscar came out in the fourth round and hit his opponent with what was his giant-killer – an explosive right hand. The fellow dropped to the mat instantly, with a hint of seizure activity on the way down.

Fact is, I thought my Oscar had killed him. Luckily, the bandage had held.

———

On the same day I drained Oscar de la Hoya's thigh abscess and allowed him to fight in his first nationally-televised prize fight, I saw nine other patients, all Medicare or doubly eligible for Medicare and Medicaid, the program for the poor.

None of those nine bills were paid, as the federal contractors denied all or part of the payments as "not covered by Medicare" because of billing regulations.

I wrote and called the federal experts to ask how they should have been billed, and was told that they could not teach me how to bill Medicare, only respond if someone complained about my billed services as a fraud suspect.

Top Rank Boxing, of course, paid my bill immediately, then Arum asked me to quit my practice and become Oscar's private doctor at double whatever my current income was.

Bob Arum said he would reserve the top suite in Caesar's Palace for my wife and myself at Oscar's next fight, so that I could begin my new role as personal physician to the future world champion in four weight divisions.

I wished them well and politely declined.

CHAPTER 5

Benjie, the Hairless Chihuahua

*"Mama's skin was bright yellow, the color of jaundice,
indicating severe liver failure."*

THE CALL CAME IN EARLY IN THE DAY from an Italian family living in the South Bay area of San Diego.

"Mama's a-dying and don't wanna eat anymore," said Rosalie, the daughter, over the phone. She said her 80-year-old Mother had been sick for months and hadn't been out of bed for six weeks. She had refused to go to the hospital in the past, but now was unable to talk.

My partner Jim and I walked into the small home together shortly thereafter. We never even had to ring the doorbell. Rosalie and her two sisters, Maria and Francesca, were waiting outside, distraught.

"Mama no a-eat. She a-goin to-a die, I know it!" said Maria.

One look at Mama told me she was right.

The elderly woman lay motionless on her back on a queen-sized bed, naked except for a hand-sewn quilt drawn up above her breasts. I pulled the quilt down to her waist as Rosalie, Maria, and Francesca crowded around the bed in the small 8×10 foot bedroom.

The entire perimeter of the ceiling was shelved and housed what must have been a valuable collection of beautiful dolls in handmade costumes, all covered in plastic. The dolls seemed to be looking down at us, much like med students over the operating theatre at Mass General Hospital, where anesthesia was introduced 160 years ago.

Mama's skin was bright yellow, the color of jaundice, indicating severe liver failure. In the corner of the small room, under a 20-inch tall doll neatly dressed in a pearl-studded bridal gown, was a large pile of empty vodka bottles. Maria saw my frown.

"Mama a-been-a drinker all her life," she said. "It's-a the only pleasure she-a got anymore."

She was pulseless with a swollen protuberant abdomen that had huge vessels striating across it, a result of portal hypertension when alcoholism has scarred the liver too much for blood to pass through easily.

"Well, would you like me do some blood tests on her liver to see how bad it is?" I suggested.

I had already decided that if they were in agreement, this was a patient who had had her run, and the sisters indicated all they wanted to know was "How soon?"

Jim took the blood out to the van to test her liver and kidney function, rough indicators of her imminent demise. Suddenly, I realized I had nothing to do. I was left sitting on a stool by the bed in an 8x10 foot bedroom with a near-dead alcoholic woman surrounded by her three histrionic Italian daughters.

The 40 dolls, immaculately coiffed and dressed in their finest, looked down at me critically and completed the not-quite Norman Rockwell scene.

It was an off-putting feeling, but was soon replaced by another awkward event. I had pulled the patients' quilt back over her naked breasts, but there appeared to be a stirring under the quilt down above her other private parts.

Quickly, I pulled the quilt all the way off, and there, sitting on the patient's mons veneris, was a tiny, brown, hairless chihuahua. His eyes were red, weeping pus and bugged out in a most frightful manner. As he blinked repeatedly, it was obvious he had a purulent conjunctivitis that must have been painful.

"Oh, a Benji is-a so sick!" screamed Francesca.

"Benji stop-a eating when Mama no talka to him no more," wailed Maria.

"He's no mov-a from Mama for five days," lamented Rosalie.

"Benji's a-gonna die!" they all cried in unison.

Suddenly, the room was filled with the sorrowful tears of three Italian ladies, who seemed to have forgotten all about their Mama in the throes of Benji's pain.

"Well," I said furtively. "I think Benji just has conjunctivitis and it might hurt his eyes to eat when he moves his jaw. I have some eye drops that will stop the pain and antibiotics that should cure his infection if you like."

You would have thought the sisters had just won the lottery.

They started screaming with joy, their tears from Mama's imminent demise replaced by tears of happiness. As I put the eyedrops in, Benji blinked appreciatively, never moving from his Mama's naked crotch.

"Maria," screamed Rosalie, who appeared to be the group leader. "Quicka, go getta some of that raw hamburger we were-a saving for Mama's dinner!"

Maria scrambled over me, being unable to move the stool in any direction due to the narrow space on the left side of Mama's bed. In a flurry of activity that made our emergency room CPR look slow, Maria returned with a huge bowl full of raw meat and placed it directly on Mama's barely-hirsute, but naked pubis.

Benji dove into the meat bowl balanced on her crotch head first, standing on Mama's big yellow belly with his wagging tail in the direction of her comatose head. He must have been famished.

The redness of Benji's eyes was already receding when Jim returned ceremoniously and stopped at the narrow door near the head of the bed. He held the lab results gravely in his hand, a quixotic look on his face.

The women were still laughing, crying, celebrating the great medical breakthrough of Benji's new ability to eat, now speaking all at once in Italian phases that sounded like joy. Jim stood stunned at the door.

He looked at me, I looked silently at him. The three overjoyed sisters looked at each other. The well-dressed dolls all looked sternly down on us. Benji looked only at the red meat his face was plunging into, again and again.

"Don't ask" was all I said to Jim. He handed me the lab slip.

Jim, ever sensitive to the many unforeseen events that occur in a house call practice, stood dignified and silently at the door while I interpreted the ominous, non-survivable lab results to the three sisters.

Mama, for her part, never moved a muscle. The sisters were ecstatic.

"Benji's A-GONNA LIVE!" they all cried out.

As we walked out to the Mobile Physician Treatment Center for an obvious de-briefing, I noticed a smirk edging from the corner of Jim's mouth.

With a barely suppressed chuckle as we got in the van, he said: "Can't wait to hear the story."

PART 2

Lights and sirens

CHAPTER 6

The man who wouldn't die

"There is no higher rank than being a war hero."

AT 4 IN THE MORNING ON AUGUST 15, 1945, it must have been stinking hot on the *USS Archerfish* as she silently glided through the Sea of Japan.

Submerged at periscope depth and running at flank speed with hot electric motors in the warm coastal waters, the crew were primed and ready to fight. It had been a frustrating war cruise so far, with no chance to launch their deadly torpedoes despite several enemy ship sightings.

Some of the crew suspected their Captain was either unlucky, or simply reluctant to pull the trigger. They all knew that 25% of submariners had never returned from their stealthy duties in WWII, so it was essential for crew morale that you at least got a chance to fire on the hated enemy.

All night long they had been chasing a ship they had found simply by chance, not knowing it represented Japan's last real hope in competing against the Allies on the high seas. At their first periscope sighting, the ship was so big the officers in the conning tower had thought it was an island.

But it was moving!

After flash-messaging an outline of its shape to the Pentagon intelligence officers by encrypted radio waves, they received the famous message in return: "Sink it!"

What Capt. Enfield and the officers of Archerfish didn't know was this ship was the *Shinano*, the largest vessel ever built at that time. It was so big there wasn't a drydock in the world large enough to build it, so the Japanese had strung camouflage netting between two mountains and dug out the valley in between.

When the time came, they had cut a channel letting in the Sea of Japan, and the super-carrier was launched. It was carrying over a hundred fighter planes and thousands of crew intent on killing Americans.

Tonight was its maiden cruise, and it had run smack into the frustrated men of the *USS Archerfish*.

Fortunately for the Allies, the First Officer on the diesel submarine was Lieutenant Commander "Bobo" Bobyczynski, a man Captain Enfield had learned to trust. After making his initial decision to plot a course which would have prevented closing within torpedo range of the fast-moving *Shinano*, Captain Enfield fortunately listened to the arguments of LCDR Bobyczynski.

"Bobo" pointed out that *Shinano* would probably zig where Capt. Enfield had predicted a zag following the random course changes of wartime. Capt. Enfield deferred to his First Officer, and a few hours later all six torpedoes struck the world's largest warship, sending it and its men to the bottom of the sea.

———

As a Navy brat and career Navy physician, such stories have always been captivating to me. I never lose sight of the privilege I feel when taken into a patient's confidence.

Sometimes, the non-medical factors in a patient's life are as important as the medical ones.

When treating war heroes, taking a history will often put the patient in a special category in my mind. We have a saying in the military: "Rank has its privilege," but there is no higher rank than being a war hero.

Decades after the *Archerfish* sank the *Shinano*, I had the honor of making my first formal house call on the now "Captain-retired" Sigmund Alfred Bobczynski.

To me, he became simply "The Man Who Wouldn't Die."

———◦◦◦———

Then merely a second-year surgery resident, I had attempted to remove a cyst from Bobo's left earlobe after purloining some equipment and supplies from the Navy Hospital in San Diego.

In one of those mysterious quirks of fate so common in both the Navy and in medicine, I had recently run into his son in San Diego, who also happened to be my best childhood friend back in Norfolk, Virginia.

It seemed reasonable to drop by his father's house and exercise my then-mediocre surgical talents and poor judgment by attempting to remove the cyst as the Captain lay stoically on his kitchen table.

As the more mature surgeon might have anticipated, without proper lighting and the advantages of a minor operating suite, I ruptured the cyst and the wound became infected. I began making daily house calls to pack the wound and assuage my guilt for good intentions gone awry.

What amazed me from this poor surgical outcome was the intense gratitude the Captain had for not having to wait in a typically overwhelmed surgical clinic. He asked me to become "his doctor."

Becoming "his doctor" was vastly different than him becoming "my patient."

By reversing the direction of care, I had, through no genius of my own, created a hidden value of restoring the trust in the patient/ doctor relationship. I was a guest in his home each time I visited, so I knew he wanted me to come.

Every time I came to the front door, he let me in, and he never missed his appointments.

Furthermore, he knew I valued him as a patient, because I kept coming back to do what I could to solve his ailments.

Over the next two decades, the Captain had developed a number of serious medical problems, born of a life at sea, ill-nourished by cigarettes, and dictated by unfortunate genetic markers. His house was on my way home from work, so it was natural to drop by and manage these problems.

On one of these routine calls, I asked him if his chest pain was any different in its nature or frequency. I had lately been controlling his angina with the usual drugs.

He said, "No," but his wife, eavesdropping from the next room, apparently thought differently.

"That's not true, honey," she said kindly but emphatically. "It's now waking you up at night."

What's known as the Prinzmetal's variant of angina is life-threatening, so I admitted him to the hospital as an emergency case for his cardiologist.

Two weeks later, the Captain got his four-vessel bypass for unstable angina. He began a difficult recovery in the hospital, later compounded by a profound depression that even his devoted family could not penetrate.

Again, I was challenged with repeated house calls the function of which often seemed to be more observation than therapy. I found myself making decisions in a vacuum. No nurses validated my vital signs, no consultants walked down his halls.

I asked my hospital's Ethics Committee to review my charts, but they said the house call practice had no standing under their hospital-based rules.

Thus was I alone at sea without a compass, and the U.S. healthcare system appeared much larger than the *Shinano*.

CHAPTER 7

Now completely blue

"He had been a long time without a heartbeat or oxygen."

THE CAPTAIN CONTINUED TO DEVELOP one serious medical problem after another. He suffered from transient ischemic attacks (TIAs, or mini-strokes), recurrent heart attacks, a rhythm disturbance requiring a pacemaker, and kidney failure requiring dialysis.

During these episodes, I continually marveled at the strength of his faith.

A devoted Catholic, he feared nothing, wholly convinced his Lord would determine the best outcome for both him – and me. He said he trusted me, even though I told him we were often doing things that had never before been done in the home, like elective cardioversion.

That's one of several procedures to treat an abnormally rapid or irregular heart rate, using electricity or drugs to regain a normal and healthier heart rate.

When thinly-veiled criticism from local doctors reached me through various circuitous routes, the Captain reminded me how the house calls had saved his life, several times.

After a particularly favorable showing of our service on NBC's Today morning show, one doctor obviously fortified by spirits called me at home to make his anonymous accusation: "What do you think you're doing, measuring a potassium level in the patient's home? You can't do that!"

———⁘———

The Captain reminded me I had been doing it with our government-certified, FDA-approved portable lab device for years.

Our house call practice steadily expanded, eventually to have satellite programs started in eleven other cities. As a result, I was spending less time in hospital emergency rooms and more time in executive board meetings, where I was usually the only person in the room I had never heard of.

Of course, the modest reimbursement paid by Medicare for home visits, priced at $40 to $52 in 1996, required that I keep my "other" job, working in the ER to pay the mortgage.

A typical Friday was spent during the day making seven to ten house calls followed by a nap from 4 pm to 6 pm, followed by a 12-hour shift in the Scripps Trauma Center. It was exhausting, but the contrast in seeing so many ER patients who were clearly not as sick as my house call patients was invaluable.

I knew what their ER bills looked like. The ER paid me about four times what Medicare paid me for house calls, including lab and other services as needed. Yet, our Call Doc model, vetted by the best minds on Wall Street, showed a profitable business once we scaled up to capacity.

———⁘———

One night, I exchanged duties with a partner to work his shift in the Scripps ER. About ten minutes after entering the hospital, I heard that awful alarm followed by "Code Blue, Code Blue, 4 West, Room 423."

I ran to the room to find the staff feverishly working to revive an elderly dialysis patient who had been found dead sitting in his chair. The patient was now completely blue. He had gone a long time without a heartbeat or oxygen. The Code Team lifted him to the crash board and began CPR.

As I removed the therapist's mask to begin inserting the tube to supply oxygen through his airway, I suddenly recognized the Captain. He was in the hospital to revise yet another complication from the shunt used for his dialysis. I knew the Captain had signed a "Do Not Resuscitate" form for my house call practice and wouldn't want to live as a vegetable, so I delayed placing a tube in his windpipe.

Just as I ordered the Code Blue team to stop CPR, the nurse shouted, "All clear," and shocked his heart back to life. His pacemaker clicked in and his blood pressure became normal. Yet, he was comatose and apparently had been without oxygen to his brain for at least 20 minutes.

He appeared lifeless, lying there amidst the detritus of a "successful" resuscitation, obviously brain dead.

I called his wife and explained the unfortunate result. She graciously thanked me for "being there." After asking her to return to the hospital, I went back to his room to hear his labored respirations despite neck positioning and suction. The Captain and I had discussed such matters before, and I knew he would want to take his last breaths without obstruction if possible.

I started to intubate him again only to find that the cause of the arrest was a huge piece of veal wedged in his throat, the so-called "café-coronary" when the so-called "café" was a modern hospital.

My actions had apparently delayed any chance he might have had for an intact survival and condemned him to the very thing he feared most: living out his life as a burden to his family.

There are few things that can shake a veteran of a decade in major trauma centers, but this event did. I left orders for his wife to come see me as soon as she arrived and went back down to the relative solace of my busy emergency room, where few people die and almost nobody is that sick.

Thirty minutes later, a nurse brought incredible news. The Captain was sitting up and asking, for the first time in a year, to be taken to the dialysis he hated so much. After my ER shift, I went up to his room and confessed what had happened. He looked at me with vague interest and simply said, "Remarkable, isn't it?"

———⁓⁓⁓———

Eventually, The Man Who Wouldn't Die did elect to stop his dialysis.

His hulking frame was soon reduced to a shell that had to be carried from bed to commode and back. After a week, I measured his blood urea toxin level. It exceeded 120 (normal is 10-20), the highest level my portable lab instrument could record. I told his wife the end was near.

Two days later, she asked me to come down for a visit.

When I arrived, the Captain was sitting at the counter having a lively conversation with his wife, teaching me yet another humbling lesson in the limitations of modern medicine.

Eventually, Capt. Bobczynski's uremia increased still further, and he finally weakened too much to leave his bed, speaking little but appearing to understand everything.

One day, his wife called me urgently and asked me to come to the house. That was all the history I needed. I had told his seven children to gather round that week, that even The Man Who Wouldn't Die was bound to meet his Maker soon. His wife met me at the door.

Wordlessly, she led me down a darkened hall to his room.

The Captain lay covered in woolen shawls, no doubt reflecting on some of his many world-wide journeys.

Most of the children were there in the crowded room. Nobody spoke.

Normally, this is the time in the hospital where I respectfully excuse myself and tell the family that my nurse will take care of anything they needed. Instead, I found myself kneeling beside his bed, babbling about how grateful I was for the role he had played in my life, for everything he had taught me.

Through the intimacy of home care medicine, I had learned how not to tell patients what was best for them. But rather to inform them of their choices, describing the likely risks as well as benefits of the various procedures recommended within the so-called "standard of care."

I had learned how to make house calls using all aspects of the environment in which patients lived and dealt with their conditions.

I had learned that people of faith don't fear death; they face it with the expectation of a fantastic journey to come.

I had learned the wonderful feeling of respect and trust that family doctors in years past must have known.

Perhaps most importantly, I had begun to appreciate how instrumental my objective, but non-directive counsel could be. Even so, I learned how weak a force it was when compared to the trust and faith this devout man found in his God.

Almost unnoticed, the Captain's right index finger slowly and repeatedly flexed, drawing me nearer. It was the only movement I saw him make that last day. I leaned over the bed, kissing him on the temple, my ear close to his mouth.

"You did a good job," was the only thing he said.

Those were his last words to me.

I went home, sobbing at the memory of this great WWII hero, this Man Who Wouldn't Die who had infused in me such a passion for home visits that I knew we must teach others about the value of comprehensive care in the home.

CHAPTER 8

His favorite cardigan sweater

"I am so glad you called. He is not doing well."

WHEN FAMOUS PEOPLE ASK FOR A HOUSE CALL, it suggests the health-care system we have in America is falling short. Why in the world would sick people with unlimited wealth call a heretic doctor they have never met in an urgent situation?

Yet, they did call, and frequently.

———

Dr. Benjamin Spock, hero to three generations for different reasons, was one such patient I cared for in his time of need.

Dr. Spock began his public career as author of *The Common Sense Book of Baby and Child Care* in 1946. The book quickly sold 50 million copies in over three dozen languages and is still regarded as the "Baby-care Bible."

Heralded for giving parents of the Greatest Generation the right to spank their children, the Baby Boomers for his anti-war rhetoric during Vietnam, and the Generation X for his views on nuclear non-proliferation, this national icon had been reduced in 1998 to a semi-comatose, bed-bound, slowly dying old man who was shuttled in and out of the hospital.

One day, a compassionate home health nurse (*all* home health nurses in my experience are compassionate) suggested to his wife that I be called instead of having him sent back to the ER.

I arrived shortly thereafter to find Dr. Spock non-responsive, being fed through a tube inserted into his stomach through his abdominal wall, unable to speak, but able to groan weakly to noxious stimuli.

By this time, his wife trusted only his lifelong professional partner and co-author, a pediatrician in Boston. Such relationships made it obligatory to call him for "authorization" of my care plan.

After publication of his 1946 eponymous treatise *Baby and Child Care*, one of the best-selling books in history, those of my generation were raised as "Spock Babies."

Some "boomers" had convinced Dr. Spock in 1970 to run for President under the People's Party with a platform that included free universal healthcare. If he were alive today, his name would likely be Bernie Sanders.

It seemed odd calling a pediatrician in Boston to get routine approval to treat a geriatric, bedbound patient in San Diego, but it made his wife comfortable.

Besides, Dr. Spock's problems, including heart failure, peptic ulcers, a series of strokes and the myriad of problems associated with being bedridden could always be improved by consultation.

I knew it would be unlikely he would need hospitalization under my care, a radical change for his wife, so I became close to both her and their Boston pediatrician.

Still, I was not to be the only doctor for Dr. Spock during his last year of life.

—◦◦◦—

Dr. Deepak Chopra, the New Age "alternative medicine" advocate, had come to San Diego with a million-dollar annual guarantee from Sharp Hospital. The constant infusion of his wellness concepts in the care of a critically-ill patient proved to be a constant problem for me.

On one scheduled visit, I waited 45 minutes in the front hall watching two Ayurvedic therapists chant as they moved both of his arms slowly through a passive range of motion exercise. There was one such Chopra devotee chanting on each arm as they worked on the semi-conscious Dr. Spock.

I had a brief thought of King Louis XIV, who was reputed to have two ophthalmology specialists: one for the left eye and one for the right.

In one of my earlier urgent house calls to see Dr. Spock, I had to place an intravenous line in his veins to correct a critical serum sodium level caused by rice-water tube feedings ordered by the acclaimed holistic "healer" who never called me.

With each routine visit, the interim history was the same. His ever-cheerful wife would tell me he was doing well and that "he even took a walk with me this morning." I could never figure out what that meant until the day I arrived to find Dr. Spock actually "taking his walk."

That meant the nearly comatose Dr. Spock was lifted to an erect posture from the front by a muscular aide while his wife "walked" behind him kicking his legs one after the other to simulate their "daily walk." Such is the visual power of treating patients in their home.

On another occasion, after yet another electrolyte problem from the rice-water diet that I couldn't dissuade his wife from using, repeat blood tests using the iSTAT showed an unexpected drop in his serum osmolality and acute, congestive heart failure.

After correction with intravenous fluids and diuretics, I told her we should get her husband weighed daily. A weight increase of four pounds in such patients is often an early warning of fluid retention from a failing heart.

Typically, we put four cheap, bathroom scales under the four bedposts and weighed the patient with the same bed clothes and linens at the same time each morning. I wasn't overly concerned what his actual weight was, only to detect notable weight gain from a baseline when he was not in heart failure.

A few weeks later, Mrs. Spock proudly handed me a digital printout of his weight down to the fraction of an ounce every 15 minutes. Using his connections and wealth, she had secured a $50,000

NASCAR-certified scale used to weigh racing cars and placed his hospital bed on it.

On March 15, 1998, I was in the neighborhood running errands on a weekend and called his wife to see if I could drop by to check on Dr. Spock. With a heavily stressed voice, she nearly shouted, "Of course, I am so glad you called. He is not doing well."

I entered through the heavy oak door to find Dr. Spock pale, pulseless and unresponsive, taking shallow breaths. It was clearly his time.

His wife, after years of incredible support and "daily walks," was very diligent, yet had never been clear to me about his end-of-life directive. Usually, patients like this are in a "Do Not Resuscitate" status, but I sensed that she favored a "Full Court Press," perhaps influenced by his publisher and the upcoming release of his final papers in a last, soon-to-be-published book.

—◦◦◦—

A full court press typically starts with a 911 call, followed by lights and sirens alerting the neighborhood, paramedic intubation on scene followed by life support in the hospital, all futile for Dr. Spock by any criterion for a rational outcome.

Studies show that 80% of Americans want to die at home, yet only 20% get their wish.

Despite decades of hospice care being available, 60% still die in the sterile atmosphere of an acute care hospital at great cost, while the 20% who die in nursing homes seldom have the privacy of an intact family surrounding them.

Only 20 percent of us die at home, and we are usually found dead at the time.

This sanitization of death in America has significant social implications beyond the scope of this book, but you should know that there is almost nothing physicians and nurses do for dying patients in a hospital that we cannot do better in the home, where the patient is surrounded by the family and other loved ones.

To give a very nervous Mrs. Spock something useful to do, I had her inject a salt solution into his gastrostomy tube, as I began drawing blood to measure the electrolytes I knew would be out of whack. I used my iSTAT to measure his blood gases and electrolytes, showing yet again a life-threatening reduction in his serum sodium from the rice-water diet.

The activity of doing something calmed his wife, and she started to seem comfortable with his imminent demise. She was ambivalent, as usual, when I informed her about calling 9-1-1, the usual standard of care in such situations.

As reality set in, she casually mentioned that Dr. Spock had always enjoyed sitting by the fireplace in his favorite cardigan sweater. It seemed quite important to her, so I asked her to get his sweater.

Together, we put Dr. Benjamin Spock in his favorite cardigan sweater and carried him to his chair in the family room by the fireplace.

There, with both of us pushing saline solution into his gastrostomy tube for a couple of hours, we chatted about his life, his legacy, his incredible contributions to society, and the celebration that would be appropriate for his passing.

We did not talk about intubating him, or starting a dopamine drip to increase his blood pressure, or other standard resuscitation procedures. It just seemed inappropriate.

Mrs. Spock gradually adjusted to the realization that it was, indeed, his time. Together, the three of us enjoyed an intimate moment that she will cherish and I will remember as Dr. Spock quietly slipped away.

CHAPTER 9

Absolutely no negatives

"A secret group of thought leaders was formed."

OUR FINANCIAL BACKERS HAD FELT SO STRONGLY about the value we represented to society they had authorized $50,000 to hire President Reagan's Under Secretary of Health and Human Services.

Secretary David B. Swope, who had gone to seminary school before entering government service, quickly warmed to our challenge: Getting Medicare to pay for house calls in accordance with the law.

With his contacts and universally appealing reputation, we presented our concept in many of the highest offices in the land, including Senate President Bob Dole, HHS Secretary Louis Sullivan, Vice President Dan Quayle and over 30 congressional representatives.

I had personal meetings with the Director of Medicare from each of the past five Administrations, presenting the concept of house calls to increase access for complex patients with multiple chronic diseases as a way to save money. I had always been received with respect and gratitude. But nothing happened. For years.

Clearly, fixing Medicare with such a new concept simply wasn't a pressing priority, even though high-ranking medical experts heaped praise on the idea.

I recall meeting in the White House with Secretary Sullivan's Chief Health Care Policy Advisor, Gail Wilensky, PhD, who told me: "I have never heard such a great healthcare proposal with absolutely no negatives. It is just too bad we must concentrate all our efforts right now on preventing a vote on a measure President Bush [41] will have to veto."

Frustrated by failed attempts to create legislation, or even regulatory change supporting house call payments in the 1980s and '90s, the board of the nonprofit American Academy of Home Care Physicians (AAHCP) was having the same issue.

As the only member of the AAHCP Board of Directors making payroll from house call revenues, I petitioned this well-connected, influential group of salaried, academic professors who were equally committed to physician home care.

Fortunately, they were much more adept at political interactions than I was and much more connected to mainstream medicine. Most extraordinary, they were also willing to donate their time and expertise to the effort of payment reform.

A secret group of thought leaders was formed and began meeting under the tutelage of Jim Pyles, an experienced healthcare lobbyist and attorney in Washington.

In 1991, the AAHCP Board became convinced that if we didn't get doctors adequately paid by Medicare for making house calls we probably had no rationale for existence ... or future membership. The board's members threw their personal efforts and reputations behind the cause.

As an added bonus, my venture capital backers had authorized a $150,000 donation to the non-profit AAHCP over three years to buy access on Capitol Hill. Such are the requirements for input to our so-called "representational democracy."

Presto!

—◦◦◦—

A mere eight years later in 1999, Medicare began what they said was appropriate payment for the work and practice expense of making home visits.

A little-known fact was that of the physicians who completed the

National Survey Instrument required by Medicare to create new payment codes for home visits, more than half were employed by the house call programs we had started in San Diego.

Even less understood was Medicare's refusal to pay for the time and cost of transportation to and from a patient's home to make the house call. Their entire rationale was based on the fear that physicians would abuse any travel reimbursement methodology they could implement.

Even now, the time and travel cost to a physician coming and going into your house is not compensated by any form of federal reimbursement. Today, the original $42 Medicare-allowed home visit fee can be as high as $234 for a complex new patient home visit.

Various other services, like bringing your own lab and equipment or covering the time and expense of driving to the patient's home are still being refused compensation—all in clear violation of the 1989 statutes requiring that Medicare compensate physicians for care that is medically reasonable and necessary.

However, the economies of scale and found benefits in new value-based payment schemes have led to several breakout programs with a national, scalable presence. Indeed, at least three house call networks have now been purchased at prices in excess of $100 million.

Unfortunately, all three were purchased by health insurance companies, but the high valuations are still a telling statistic.

Despite the commercial success of these programs and years of research showing universal savings at 15 sites, we are still waiting for Medicare to bring the concept to everyone by allowing any qualified mobile physician to participate.

But be patient … pun very intended.

CHAPTER 10

No matter where you die

"She was pulseless, dying a horrible, suffocating death."

I WAS IN MRS. PRICE'S UPSTAIRS BEDROOM late one Friday night in 1990, pushing intravenous drugs into her swollen forearm with growing desperation. She was 85 and dying.

She was vomiting blood, aspirating, coughing, struggling, unable to speak being so short of breath, obviously close to death. Her soiled nightgown and bedsheets had the stale smell of human degradation. As a critical care physician, I was supposed to relieve her suffering, but the drugs were not working.

Cancer sucks, no matter where you die.

Her husband and son were arraigned quietly in the bedroom, anxiously hoping I would create order out of this chaos. All three of them had trusted me explicitly during her prior years of Call Doc, up to the point when I told her it was pointless to seek further care for her metastatic melanoma.

Now, she was *in extremis*, back from a world-famous cancer center with her liver swollen by tumor, her entire body puffy from the inability to make, or keep, proteins in her blood, her clotting mechanisms ruined by chemotherapy more hopeless than hopeful.

The melanoma was always going to kill her, but she had now lost control of any semblance of comfort after various experimental treatments from the cancer specialists ruined the few weeks of health she might have had left.

Her skin was a toxic yellow from a tumor-filled liver's inability to detoxify her blood. She was pale, signifying internal bleeding caused by experimental chemotherapy. Nausea from blood in her stomach forced her to sit up, but her weak heart couldn't pump against the additional gravity.

She was pulseless, dying a horrible, suffocating death in her second floor bedroom. Nobody said a word.

The last time I had seen her, she wasn't jaundiced, short of breath, or even showing signs of the silently growing tumors in her liver and lungs. It had been during a house call to her well-known husband, chairman of a prestigious investment banking firm in San Diego.

In a miracle of coincidences, he provided initial funding for what became my $30 million venture-backed effort to bring back physician house calls, making me notorious if not famous, but proud of being called "The Father of House Calls" by board members of the non-profit Academy of Home Care Physicians.

Mrs. Price (not her real name) had come into the living room as I examined her husband, asking me if I could explain an unusual belly pain that she had developed recently.

Knowing her history included a rare melanoma found on her retina, and that she had chosen cobalt radiation (90% effective) rather than removal of the eye (100% curative), I made her lie down to feel her liver, where melanoma goes to kill us. Her liver was huge, knobby, full of tumor, the kiss of death.

In 1990, there was no potential treatment for metastatic melanoma like there is now with the recent genetic advances, so I pleaded with them both to decline further treatment in her final few weeks of life.

But some forces, like the vanity which saved her eye but not her life, or the well-feeling patient's desire for a full court press are simply more powerful than advice from a trusted doctor, even one that makes house calls.

They had ignored me.

Now she was rapidly dying, a victim of our universal will to live and an oncologist's never-ending bag of tricks. Instead of a cruise to the Caribbean, she had flown to a famous cancer center, where her husband's connections no doubt secured her the most advanced and most expensive care available at the time.

All they could offer her in 1989 were poisons to attack her tumor (hopefully) and every other cell in her body (for sure).

Mrs. Price had absorbed all the narcotics I carried in my black bag. There was still no relief for her gasping respirations. Her 80-year-old husband of many years and grown son sat as quietly frantic observers.

In the more customary hospital setting of the ICU or emergency room, I would simply have written nursing orders for "2-6 mg morphine IVP [intravenous push] as needed for relief of symptoms" and fabulous nurses would have made sure she was comfortable.

Hours or days later, I would have gotten the call that my patient had died; then I would call the husband. And that's that.

However, trying to earn the moniker "Father of House Calls" on this Friday night in a second-story bedroom six blocks from my home, I didn't even have time to put in an intravenous line, much less get a second opinion. She was gasping, agonizingly short of breath, and bleeding to death right in front of me.

Another gastric eruption covered us both in coffee ground (dried blood) emesis.

I know the smell. It will come home with me. Usually, this is a problem for the ER nurses to deal with…not the doctor.

Even though they had not sought my services since leaving town in their "search for the cure," I found myself there by a stubborn insistence on a simple, revolutionary concept: comprehensive care in the home setting. After all, they had called me that night and refused 9-1-1 because they knew I would come.

Her comfort, and death, were now my problem.

The multiple intravenous injections of Demerol®, then morphine, were not working. I was out of opiates, and the only sedative I had left was a 10 milligram vial of a potent, but highly variable sedative called Versed®. If I titrated it at the customary milligram-at-a-time dosage, I would lose its maximum potential effect and run the risk of not ever relieving her suffering.

If I gave it to her all at once, she might stop breathing.

Every other doctor in America would have called 9-1-1. In fact, they would have insisted the patient's family call 9-1-1 earlier that Friday night when the family called me at home, *in extremis.*

—*◦◦◦*—

We all know what would have happened had modern "U.S. Healthcare" taken over. The 9-1-1 scenario is a miracle for the few, but tragic for many. A "lights-and-sirens" ambulance transport costing over $2,000 would have pulled up, yanked her onto a gurney, and driven screaming (the ambulance, that is) to the "nearest appropriate facility," meaning "closest emergency room."

Since her internist kept her records at a hospital 8 miles farther away, the three closer hospitals would not have had her records, known her story, or been able to personalize her care. In other words, the ER doctor that received her couldn't have been sure she was dying, yet the horse had already left the barn.

Such patients seldom arrive with written charts in tow.

Under California SB 125, paramedics must take you to the "nearest appropriate" facility, often resulting in one that doesn't have your records, where your doctor doesn't have privileges, and is therefore, a place where you likely don't want to go.

This way, a complete, duplicate work-up with labs and CT scans is justified by the ER doctor, who rarely has time to call your primary care physician in an emergency. At this point, the patient can rapidly become a victim of modern medicine.

Our San Diego studies report that nearly 90% of patients in such ambulances "don't need immediate physician attention."

However, duplicated ER studies, billed at the highest charges we have in the emergency room, are good for business. A quarter of hospital admissions come through the ER, disproportionately more in the elderly age groups.

Such is the state of U.S. healthcare, a $3.2 trillion industry that really doesn't want to change.

———✦———

What is good for the patient is often bad for profits.

In the emergency room, if not on the way in the ambulance, Mrs. Price would have been sedated preventing an accurate history if it was even possible for her to give one, intubated (so she couldn't talk), placed on life support, and possibly even transfused with blood if the husband or son took too long to follow up with her medical history.

Some $22,000 later (a typical San Diego resuscitation charge for such patients), she would have been admitted despite the hopelessness of her situation.

How could they possibly grasp the full implication of Mrs. Price's history with a metastatic melanoma from an un-operated tumor in the back of her eyeball five years earlier, now afflicted by complications from world-famous, well-meaning oncologists in Dallas, Texas?

Answer: They couldn't.

PART 3

Mobile tools

CHAPTER 11

Too dumb to understand

*"It is malpractice to think you can do
a potassium level in the home!"*

I WAS IN HER BEDROOM on a Friday night, with no other objective or trained medical personnel in the room with me, just the family.

I stuck another needle into another vein and blasted the 10 mg of Versed® into her all at once.

Mrs. Price immediately stopped breathing.

The room was transformed into peacefulness as quickly as her crisis must have started an hour earlier when her husband called me. In the awkward silence, I began saying the Lord's Prayer. The family joined in.

Then, they thanked me profusely for being there, for being available, for being nearby, for having the foresight to carry powerful medications, for having the skill to give intravenous injections, for avoiding the "lights and sirens," but mostly for just knowing what to do.

I called the coroner to document her medical death, the family's choice for decedent affairs to pick up her body, and left without telling the family of my internal conflict.

Did I really deserve such praise? What they didn't know was that under the laws of the State of California at the time, I could have been tried for murder.

Back in 1990, a malpractice action against me would have been successful at the very least. Malpractice liability is based upon comparing your actions to what is called "the community standard of care."

Making house calls with a crash cart, oxygen and a pharmacy in the van parked in Mrs. Price's driveway was anything but the community standard of care.

Although this sort of death happens all the time in the more controlled, witnessed cluster of a hospital room, the mere prospect of having to defend my actions alone in her bedroom that night worried me. The applicable laws are still archaic and will never catch up to what we can do with modern technologies in the privacy of the home setting.

Although California has recently followed Oregon and Hawaii with laws condoning physician-assisted suicide, these laws would not have provided any protection in Mrs. Price's situation. With physician-assisted suicide, patients are required to inject their own medications following a lengthy process of approval by multiple professionals.

The truth was, Mrs. Price was just too emergently ill to allow a process for anything. She was too acutely ill to make any sort of informed decision.

—◦◦◦—

In 1990 the label "Father of House Calls" was hardly meant as a compliment. Still, I continued to get requests from doctors who thought "their" patients might want to come for an office visit when they were too sick to walk.

At the time, I had already been doing X-rays, EKGs and lab tests with a Medicare-certified, state-registered portable lab instrument in patients' bedrooms for years.

There is nothing so dangerous in a medical community as to force physicians into a discussion for which they have no ken. To them, house calls were what they did once or twice a year: stopping on the way home from the office to hold hands with a "LOL in NAD" – a little-old-lady in no-acute-distress.

It certainly wasn't making urgent responses to a dying patient's home carrying controlled substances and armed with lab and X-ray capability in a $350,000 van parked outside.

Most doctors are just too busy to keep up with new technological innovations, but I was also too dumb to understand the political and social ramifications of starting a private house call practice that made every other private physician "look bad."

This was before managed care changed the concept of private practice, and the majority of physicians became salaried. Doctors back then were intensely protective of their patients, and even more possessive.

Making house calls was considered "patient stealing," a term akin to the "ambulance chaser" used for lawyers who advertised.

If you really want to piss off a doctor, even today, you put them in the position of having to answer a patient's question concerning a topic they know nothing about ... but think they do.

Unfortunately, that was what I was doing by re-introducing the house call with modern technology. Worse yet, after the first house call to new patients, over 80% of them dumped their primary care physician, some dating back more than 40 years and begged me to become their personal physician.

I soon realized I was going to need a major capital investment to meet the demand, as well as learn how to practice geriatric medicine.

CHAPTER 12

Trying to relieve her suffering

"There's a doctor making house calls in San Diego who gives me grave concerns."

CLEARLY, I HAD A LOT TO LEARN about bringing emergency care into the home. Yet, I was board-certified in emergency medicine, trained in critical care, had mastered the surgical procedures, and had already been making house calls for some years.

Still, Mrs. Price presented the first ethical conundrum I had ever faced.

Suffice to say, her family was most grateful. I was invited to the funeral, as became common in the practice, and learned to give eulogies to my patients, something few emergency physicians ever have the privilege to do. Virtually all of the patients and families loved the house call, especially in urgent situations.

Later, after our ten-physician mobile medical group was averaging 2,000 monthly house calls and had trained groups making over 350,000 house calls in eleven cities in five states, the complaint-letter file had only six entries, five from crazy people.

We knew we had to be doing something right.

Pioneer physicians bear a terrible burden of proof. The entire healthcare system is biased against change, considering any change an evil long before its fair trial. Even simple things like the sedation of dying patients – simple to physicians, that is – can become controversial when new ideas threaten established medical standards.

It took decades for the concept of palliative care to join hospice as a sub-specialty.

Back in 1990, the urgent house call was a concept we invented merely by meeting the patient's needs. As managed care invaded the practice of medicine with its bureaucracy of cost constraints, we preserved our own professional ethic by escaping through the patient's front door.

As we designed our increasingly refined delivery system of physician house calls, we approached every question the same way: What would I want to happen if I were the patient?

Soon, I heard rumor of a doctor whom I had helped train in prior years standing up as a delegate to the California State Medical Society and saying, "There's a doctor making house calls in San Diego that gives me grave concerns."

I am sure he was responding to the considerable media reports that were coming out about our practice, all of which were extremely favorable. However, despite academic credentials at the UC San Diego Medical School and experience as chairman of the world's largest military emergency department, I was still worried about my concept's lack of peer acceptance.

You see, mobile physicians find themselves in situations like no other doctor, no matter what their specialty.

Although my intensive care training in general surgery, intensive care, and emergency medicine made me both comfortable and qualified to treat Mrs. Price, it was still the fact I was doing it in her bedroom unmonitored by nurses with no third-party set of rules to guide behavior that set our practice apart.

Adapted from the AMA's Ethics Statement, the American Academy of Home Care Physician's (AAHCP) Code of Ethics provides a standard for ethical behavior, but gives little specific guidance in how to navigate situations such as Mrs. Price, nor perhaps should it.

What is needed is an ongoing, national commission to discuss the complex bioethics introduced by simply reversing the process of medicine: from the institution into the home.

It still doesn't exist.

———✺———

Years later, I ran into Dr. Fred Abrams, Chair of the Ethics Committee for the American College of OB/GYN and author of *Doctors on the Edge* (Sentient, 2006). I found myself relaying the concern I still had about the injection causing this woman's death, albeit in the setting of an imminently fatal illness.

He asked me a simple question: "When you gave that last big injection, what was the purpose that you felt in your heart? Were you trying to relieve her suffering or were you trying to kill her?"

I quickly answered, "Of course I was trying to relieve her suffering."

"Then what's the problem?" he said.

CHAPTER 13

Two possible outcomes

"The trust is implicit and usually complete."

AT THAT MOMENT, IT WAS AS IF A GIANT WEIGHT had suddenly been lifted off my soul, but over the years I continue to reflect on the complicated issues surrounding Mrs. Price's death.

Today, I recognize the problem as one involving government agencies which feel the doctor-patient relationship is their responsibility, not yours or mine.

Over the decades, and with the support of over a hundred other board-certified physicians we trained and started in mobile practices, we persisted in making house calls feeling fulfilled, if a bit smug at times.

We introduced the first mobile portable X-ray, the first EKG, the first lab tests, the first arterial blood gases, the first spinal tap, the first elective cardioversion for a-fib, the first paperless health record in the cloud, and other "firsts" that had not been done outside the hospital since the days before ambulances were introduced by World War I.

About the only tests we couldn't do in the home in minutes were things like CT or MRI imaging.

With the equipment of a hospital emergency room sans CT scanner, mobile clinicians now can practice with near-complete autonomy. When you are a guest in the patient's home, the trust is implicit and usually complete.

We quickly learned that the rationale for adopting any new portable technology was its "dispositive value."

That is, would the presence of a procedural or test result affect our decision to send the patient to a hospital or nursing home, or could they safely stay in their own bedroom?

In short, we found out that in urgent situations, what is most important to the patient is information, not transportation.

Today, the ethical questions remain complex, albeit subtle for such a radical shift in thinking. Mrs. Price's terminal sedation is now widely accepted in the hospital setting under the "principle of double effect."

If an action has two possible outcomes, one of which is negative, the intent of the person responsible for the action becomes key.

As Supreme Court Justice Sandra Day O'Connor wrote in her 1997 decision: "...a patient who is suffering from a terminal illness and who is experiencing great pain and suffering has no legal barriers to obtaining medication, from qualified physicians to alleviate the suffering, even to the point of causing unconsciousness and hastening death."

Why should the location of such care change this opinion?

CHAPTER 14

We were all scared

"Don't worry, son, we're gonna bust out of here."

THE FUTURE DEPUTY WHITE HOUSE COUNSEL suddenly swerved onto the apron beside Route 21 outside Charlotte, North Carolina.

It was dark, raining, and Vince Foster wanted to get a little more "face-time" with his date before we took the girls back to Queens College. Vince was a year older than me, but he seemed much older. We often double-dated, as I was the only frat member who didn't own a car at Davidson College.

"You drive, Gresham," Vince said. "You're too drunk to play the radio." I had been fiddling with the radio dials trying to get better reception on the long, country road after our all-day party beside Lake Norman.

It was 1968, just before the Tet Offensive began killing young boys like us in Viet Nam at wholesale rates. Things were different. You grew up in an intact family, went to college, and chose a profession which often required graduate school. You also drank way too much, and drove when you shouldn't have.

I remember walking around Vince's late-model, white Impala with red leather seats in the pouring rain. The trunk was open so the keg would fit in upright with the tap still inserted in case we needed beer refills on the 45-minute drive from the non-alcoholic Davidson campus to Queen's College in downtown Charlotte.

Despite the stormy darkness, the big red letters of "BUDWEISER" were boldly visible over the rear bumper.

Vince and I traded places. I slipped behind the wheel as Vince slipped his tongue into his pretty date's mouth. The radio blared, the big engine roared, and life was as good as it gets. Why it didn't end for me that night was a miracle.

Entering Charlotte on Route 21 before the interstate later provided beltway access, one had to go downtown through the "bad district" where the poor, black Southerners were sequestered from the privileged, college-town crackers.

It was raining so hard I could barely see, and we were late.

Speeding on the four-lane road though the center of town, we came to an unlighted underpass that narrowed the road quickly as it went beneath a bridge of some sort.

In the heavy rain, there suddenly appeared a man in a full yellow rain-suit, the kind you see on the Morton's salt shaker ads. He was standing in the middle of my lane, the fast lane, waving a light back and forth.

Without slowing down, I moved quickly over to the right lane to pass him, barely reducing speed as we raced under the bridge.

That was when the train hit us.

I never even saw it.

It came from the other side of the underpass and struck the white Impala in the right, rear, quarter panel, spinning the car around at least three times on the rain-soaked asphalt. Hit a few feet forward or going a few miles per hour slower, and we would have all been crushed.

Eventually, the car came to rest literally on the wrong side of the tracks, headlights pointed backwards through the sleeting rain. Almost instantly, dozens of young black men poured out of their own party and circled ominously around our car.

Nobody was hurt, but we were all scared.

It seemed the police cars all arrived at the same time. I don't have clear memory of this part, either from the beer or the bump on my head. I just remember feeling terrified, not grateful to be alive.

Vince and I had gotten out of the car, leaving our dates and a third couple still inside. Since nobody seemed to be injured, the problem now seemed to be a racial thing, though I wasn't sure why.

I walked over to the policeman writing out his notes and our citations, or both, and asked him what was happening.

He appeared frustrated, standing near the rear of the Impala where we both soon were saturated not only with the rain but with a heavy mist of beer spewing from the fractured keg.

"Who was driving?" was all he said to me.

"I was," I said as I contemplated what I was going to tell my father, who was living in Naples, Italy at the time.

"The witnesses say the owner of the car was driving," the cop said.

"No, I was," I sheepishly admitted, not wanting to add "liar" to my long list of infringements that night.

"Ok," the cop said. "You can both go to jail."

⸻

Later, my recollection of the memorable night became clearer as the beer haze lifted from me, but not from Vince. We were in the Charlotte Police Station jail, loosely housed in the "drunk tank" with only one other criminal: a 16-year old quivering adolescent that Vince had his arm around.

In a drunken whisper, Vince was saying to the terrified young man, "Don't worry, son, we're gonna bust out of here."

Now, there were *two* terrified adolescents in the drunk tank with President Clinton's future personal attorney.

Vince stood up shakily, whispered for me to follow him, and tiptoed through the open, barred cage doors, sliding quietly past the watch-room where the guard was supposedly supervising the inhabitants from this night's debauchery.

He was sitting with his feet up, facing the other way, browsing through a *Playboy*, one of the few details that still stands out in my cloudy memory of the events that followed.

Quickly, Vince and I started running down a long hall toward a metal door at the end which, in our ignorance, we presumed was unlocked and opened to freedom.

"Where the hell did those college drunks go?"

We heard the night guard yell soon after we got to the door which, of course, was locked. Hearing lots of rapid footsteps, Vince jumped into a side room off the hall, and I ran into another and tried to hide under a table. It turned out to be where they fingerprinted us later.

We lead our lives perilously through a jungle of events we mostly deserve, and sometimes a good outcome seems futile. Other times, we are saved by forces beyond our knowledge or control. How we are saved is not usually the more important question at the time.

Why we were saved is the question I ponder most now that I am nearing the latter third of my life.

———✐✐✐———

Even in the '60s, drunk driving was a significant blight on your personal character, as well as your driving license.

Add reckless driving, speeding, failing to yield at a train crossing, causing an accident with significant damage and the potential for "great bodily harm," and attempting to break out of jail added to my personal fears that night.

Of course, jail time could have prevented me from graduating from college, going to medical school, or starting a house call movement.

The result surprised me, until explained years later by Vince's death. The next morning, we were bailed out of jail by our fraternity brothers. At trial a few weeks later, I was briefly reprimanded by the judge and only fined $75 for "reckless driving." The fraternity paid my fine.

That was how much Vince Foster was respected even then. He was never charged with anything. I definitely should have received more punishment. Apparently, a call to the Rose Law Firm back in Hope, Arkansas made the difference.

Thirty years later, Vince Foster's body was found in Fort Marcy Park in Washington, D.C. The Deputy Counsel to President Clinton and Hillary Clinton's good friend and mentor had killed himself after six months in the White House.

Travelgate was in the news along with controversies over Whitewater real estate deals and President Clinton's decisions to admit gays openly into the military. Those events seem trivial now.

In his depressive suicide note, Vince had written that he was killing himself because he couldn't work in a place "where ruining people's lives is considered sport."

Whatever that meant.

———⟡———

It is hard to overestimate the complexity of political dynamics in Washington, and I don't propose to know the answers.

My personal calling was to bring back physician house calls as a reform that not only solved the Medicare budget crisis but restored the medical profession to a former sanctity governed by the doctor-patient relationship.

What could be more obvious than house calls as we hunker down in social isolation through the first quarter of 2020, hiding from the COVID-19 global pandemic?

Instead of a crisis in hospital beds, why is it not a crisis in finding enough mobile physicians to treat sick patients in the social isolation of their homes?

That such a pure concept in healthcare delivery has been met with only limited success speaks to the larger problems encountered by replacing medicine built upon doctor-patient trust with a market-driven trade.

The response from the thousands of patients I met in their home constantly vetted the idea.

In years of lobbying and meetings with influential congressmen and the Medicare Director under five presidential administrations, I was met with universally positive feedback, yet you still wonder how to get such services for yourself, do you not?

The steady, if slow adoption of house calls by both physicians and our political leaders is frustrating. Perhaps the astute reader will now begin asking about the Independence at Home Act of 2016, the only healthcare reform that has proven to increase access, improve care, prolong life and save taxpayer dollars.

Authorized by Section 3024 of the Affordable Care Act, what began at the Independence of Home Demonstration began in 2012 and was originally authorized for three years.

The Demonstration has shown the value of house calls for nearly a decade now, yet few people have heard of it, and few doctors believe it is truly possible to see the vast majority of patients with acute problems in the privacy of their homes.

I assure you it is possible, as soon as the public demands it – just as my father promised 35 years ago.

A doctor need make only a few house calls to patients "too sick to go to the doctor" for the light to shine on our future. It is not just the technical abilities we now have; it is the reaction from patients themselves.

You have now met some of these very special patients in this book. Someday, you likely will become one yourself. I hope your doctor will find the reward in seeing you in the intimacy of your own home.

I now know why I was saved from that should've-been-much-worse train accident and countless close calls that could've easily upended my life or career.

I must've been chosen to make house calls.

CHAPTER 15

The Great White Knight

*"Nobody wants to take care of the
demographic that's growing the fastest."*

THE PHONE RANG at about 6 in the early evening.

We were just sitting down to dinner with our son and his family. They were about to set out on a ten-day vacation to Lake Powell, re-creating the houseboat family memories of his youth.

You know, the kind of trans-generational memories that are supposed to last forever.

"Your 80-year-old patient is sitting on our living room floor," said a familiar voice. "Says he got suddenly dizzy after getting off the exercycle, and something's not right."

"I'll be right there," I said, hanging up the phone to the hopeless protest of my wife, accustomed as she was to such interruptions. I noticed neither my son nor his kids protested my leaving as they sat down to dinner.

Even in my newly-declared retirement a few years ago, they were used to it, I guess.

I arrived to find my friend Jim shirtless and sockless on the spacious living room floor, propped up against the couch. His deafness was always a problem, but he still seemed more confused than usual and had trouble picking his words.

His blood pressure was normal, but his pulse was irregular, an ominous sign for a patient prone to periodic bouts of atrial fibrillation.

His coordination was clearly off, and he was only able to stand with my help. To the uninformed, this pillar of the community would appear drunk.

A-fib will afflict at least a fourth of us older than 65, often causing a stroke despite our best attempts at anti-coagulation. It is one of those problematic conditions that is both common and frustrating, in that the treatment with blood thinners often causes the same problem for which they are prescribed: a massive stroke.

Having symptoms for less than an hour, Jim was well within the three-hour window for the magic "clot busters" used to reverse the neurological damage that can occur from a blood clot which has formed on the fibrillating atrium and broken off to lodge in the brain.

In Jim's case, he appeared to have subtle stroke signs like vigorous tendon reflexes, but didn't "lateralize," meaning there was no clear focus of problems on one side of his body or the other.

A stroke was clearly possible, but not probable.

The situation was clear to me in this zero-sum game we call emergency medicine. With the true potential of a stroke, time is of the essence, so I told his wife of some 50 years that we should call 9-1-1 to get him to the nearest stroke center.

Then I offered another option.

The UCSD Stroke Center is located at the very ER center I was recruited to after leaving active duty in the Navy in 1982. It wasn't the "nearest appropriate facility" in the eyes of a paramedic arriving by ambulance in the 10 to 12 minutes required by the City of San Diego's contract.

I knew that due to more than 20,000 delayed responses beyond acceptable contract limits, the ambulance contractor had gone bankrupt and had been replaced by the leviathan American Medical Response (AMR), a division of the Envision Health, traded on the New York Stock Exchange.

AMR now owns 80% of all the ambulances in America, contracts with thousands of hospitals for the physicians staffing their emergency rooms, and clearly is the self-declared dominant player in the pre-hospital medical care sandbox.

As such, they have been diligent in creating protocols that follow state laws, such as the one in California (SB 125) which states a paramedic ambulance must take the patient to the "nearest appropriate facility."

AMR has made billions annually for decades by enforcing protocols which promote the highly efficient (for them) use of ambulances transporting the vast proportion of patients unnecessarily for an average cost of over $1,200, one way.

Fact is, the nearest hospital is often not the hospital where the patient's records are kept, or the patient's doctor has admitting privileges, or the patient's insurance (God forbid) has a contract. In other words, it might not be the hospital to which the patient wants to go, but most patients don't know this.

When I suggested to Jim's wife that it would be reasonable for her to drive Jim to the UCSD Stroke Center, she informed me she probably shouldn't drive because she just had her eyes dilated at her eye doctor's office that afternoon.

The ability of a paramedic with only six months of community college training in healthcare to know the difference between an evolving cerebellar stroke as Jim might be having, and simple tremulousness due to an extra cup of coffee, is limited. The potential of an early or subtle stroke can easily be missed.

If the diagnosis is incorrect, the destination becomes moot to the paramedic, who likely defaults to the "nearest appropriate facility."

Having worked a decade at UC San Diego Health, one of my jobs was to be in charge of paramedic training. I also knew the drive there by heart. At this time of day, it was about 12 to 15 minutes.

As an alternative, I offered to drive Jim and his wife to the UCSD Stroke Center, calculating I could get them there before the ambulance could arrive to his house, best case.

More importantly, as a former Attending Professor of Medicine and Surgery at UCSD, I knew I could push the initial triage process and get Jim into Stroke Protocol faster.

We left Jim's house hurriedly at 6:54 pm.

Upon our arrival, the five guards at the ER ambulance ramp quickly moved to tell me, "You can't park there."

Ignoring them, I turned off the car and got out, telling them in no uncertain terms: "I'm a former Attending here and need a wheelchair for this stroke victim."

By 7:18 pm Jim had been admitted to the Stroke Protocol and was on his way to the MRI scanner. I calculated that had we called 9-1-1, Jim would've been leaving his house by ambulance about then.

Bottom line, we made it in time and Jim survived his mini-stroke with no lasting ill effects.

CHAPTER 16

Poisoned all the recruits

"Conscious enough to obey a command."

ONE SATURDAY MORNING, I was relaxing with my young daughter floating on an inner tube near the shore in San Diego Bay, when the lady who lived in the beautiful shore-front home came running out and yelled, "Are you Captain Bayne? The Admiral needs you at the hospital right now!"

I ran into her house and called my boss, who said there was a mass casualty at the Marine Corps base and hundreds of recruits seemed to be poisoned. I quickly drove home, got in uniform and raced to the Marine Corps Recruit Depot (MCRD) in my wife's beat-up VW.

As I drove to the medical clinic a large school bus full of screaming marines came careening around the corner honking loudly. I blocked the road with my car, got out and asked the panicked driver what was going on.

"I'm taking as many as I can to the hospital. Something has poisoned all the recruits!"

Looking at the wide-eyed recruits sitting and lying on the seats of the school bus, I could tell nobody was about to die by the color in their faces, so I told the driver to turn around and take everyone back to the medical clinic, which was located just across from the large, grassy parade grounds.

With the sun shining as it usually does in San Diego, we arrived in tandem at the parade grounds to see hundreds of fatigue-dressed young men sitting, lying, vomiting all over the parade grounds.

Entering the medical clinic, the fluid everywhere on the floor was slippery, a mixture of vomit, blood and bags of intravenous saline which had evidently been dropped and broken in various rooms.

The doctor, a General Medical Officer with no specialty training and just a few years out of med school, ran up to me literally screaming in a panic: "They are all sick! I think they were poisoned by a bad batch of Spam at lunch! We have to get them to the hospital as fast as possible!"

As he ran to start another intravenous on a recruit healthy enough to be sitting in a chair, it was obvious he had lost it. I noticed the sickest recruits were sitting in muck on the floor or lying down. This group all had letters in black magic markers on their foreheads: the letters "C," "D," and "A," which turned out to stand for injections given for Compazine, Demerol® and Atropine.

Pretty quickly, I figured out the sickest ones were the ones nodding their heads, barely awake.

Nobody knew the doses given and the doctor's panic had spread to the corpsmen and staff, so everybody was simply running around yelling, avoiding the Big Picture.

After stopping one more busload of recruits who looked sick but not sick enough to need hospitalization, I walked outside and counted the recruits that lying all around me, spread out across the clinic apron, the street, and the parade grounds.

There were 166 of them, and I wondered how I was going to sort out the mess.

The doctor was relieved to have help. My first order was for everyone to stop what they were doing and come to the front of the clinic for directions. It was time to begin some semblance of triage, since the DCA patients and those actively retching up bright red blood needed assessment with vital signs.

As I was wondering how I was going to do this with only three corpsmen and one dysfunctional doctor, up walked the Commandant of the Marine Corps Recruit Depot, General Woods by name.

This was fortuitous, and gave me a bright idea. General Woods, with five bands of ribbons, many indicating his command during combat in Vietnam, quietly asked me: "Doctor, tell me how I can help you."

"General, would you please call your troops to attention?" I asked.

My bright idea was to do a quick test known as "orthostatics" on everyone. Usually, this is done by taking a patient's blood pressure in a chair and seeing if it drops dramatically when standing up.

I really needed to see who was too sick to stand up out of the 166 recruits spread all around me. With only three corpsmen, it would've taken hours.

One of the most wonderful things about the military is something called "command authority," and combat Marine Corps generals have more of it than a busload of medical administrators, or doctors, for that matter.

As only a career Marine general can do, General Woods stepped up on the clinic entry steps and yelled "MARINECORPSRECRUITS, ATENNNNNNNNN-HUT!"

Still unsteady, 151 young men struggled to their feet, conscious enough to obey a command, and well enough to remain standing at parade rest for the next half-hour. That left only 15 that needed attention, plus the seven DCA flyers gorked out on the clinic floor.

The corpsmen quickly did their orthostatic vital signs, and I directed my attention to a half dozen who were, in fact, quite ill, one with a seizure unmasked by the food poisoning, and the others from, indeed, a batch of bad Spam.

The mass emergency was over, and I called my Admiral to tell him we had a total of 11 admissions coming to the hospital. They would be directly admitted to the appropriate ward, a couple to the ICU to keep the ER empty in case things deteriorated.

Never was a big fan of Spam.

PART 4

You can't do that

CHAPTER 17

A morass of complexity

*"We have seen geriatricians almost
disappear off the face of the earth."*

As Tom Cruise, Mariah Carey and 30 other celebrities found out
when embarrassing medical records were breached illegally at UCLA
Hospital in the 1990s, going to the Big House has additional risks for
the rich and famous.

When a house call doctor visits you, he/she becomes a guest in
your home, and we take that seriously, as most people would. We try
not to sit on your coffee table or in your favorite cushy chair. We either carry your chart into the house with us, or more recently, access
it in the Cloud through a secure link compliant with federal privacy
and security laws.

This was extraordinarily expensive until a few years ago, but venture capital allowed us to create a paperless, wireless network for records as early as 1999. By 2001 we had twelve full-time physicians
operating in a mobile, paperless environment because San Diego had
been selected by the Riccocet company to place fast modems on telephone poles every quarter-mile throughout the city.

This allowed us access to your medical chart wherever we were,
even driving down the road. It allowed us to use powerful new diag-
nostics that required sending electronic information to specialists for
interpretation.

We started carrying a portable machine in the late 1990s that measured cardiac output, and let patients watch their heart pump blood on a screen while a cardiologist in Texas interpreted the results for us both.

However, Riccocet went bankrupt after the dot-com disaster of 2001 and we waited ten years until true broadband existed over cellphone networks to begin anew. Today, most urban areas have fairly good wireless communications and, with various work-arounds, mobile physicians learn to use cellphones to augment their record keeping and potential for specialty consultations.

You really don't have to go to the emergency room to access high-level care anymore. Not only are there too many small house call practices to track, several national companies are rolling out with a promise in several cities to provide a doctor to your door within an hour.

This is a marked improvement from 1987, when I personally made 5% of all the complex, new patient home visits billed in Medicare in the entire country.

In 2018, Medicare recorded payment of over four million home visits, the fastest percentage growth of all types of physician encounters. It pleases me that our troops are not only increasing in number, but they are banding together.

With proper incentives, physicians can leave the vestiges of a salaried position in an overwhelmed office practice for the mobile setting, and the public will soon find their name and call for services. When servicing an urgent medical condition, the house call will cost about a tenth of the average ER charge.

All of which raises these vexing questions:

How does an office-based doctor with a known cash flow shut down their office and assume patients will call for services at home?

How does a solo doctor cross cover for urgent situations? After all, you can't be on two urgent house calls at the same time.

How does one advertise to a patient population that is too infirm to read an advertisement, and too senile to remember the ad if they could?

How does this "peasant farmer" industry of physician calls compete with the lucrative ambulance industry, which historically has been paid more for transporting you to people like me than I have ever been paid for bringing the same services to your home?

In a society engrained with the predictability of a screaming ambulance coming within 10 minutes any time you want, how does one suggest that we can no longer afford the cost when such rapid response is not necessary?

If most ambulances respond to emergencies in under 10 minutes, why is the average waiting time in U.S. emergency rooms measured in hours? What is needed is not only rapid transportation, but information at the point-of-care and time of illness.

———〰〰〰———

Years ago, I was asked to sign a contract with PacifiCare, the parent organization of a health insurance product known as Secure Horizons. With no deductible and no copay, Secure Horizons was coming to San Diego and wanted something to put on TV to attract new member to their services.

I had convinced their executives that using house calls in urgent situations would be attractive, and still save money, which was clearly their most important goal. They described to me a multi-million-dollar advertising campaign for San Diego that would feature our Mobile Physician Treatment Center racing to homes with a physician to solve their urgent problem.

I thought my dream had come true. Then I started really thinking.

These are the same brilliant executives who figured out how to suck 25% of the healthcare dollars off the top, leaving 75% for the providers to provide the care you need.

Medicare had been doing this with a fee-for-service system of 3-6% for many years. What was wrong with that picture? It just made no sense to me that managed care could save society great sums of money ... and it never has.

President Obama was even forced to cap the overhead for managed-care companies at 20% (it didn't work), while still paying 5% more per patient per year than the government would have paid under fee-for-service Medicare.

It bears repeating: Managed care has never been proven to save society money.

What it has done is create a morass of complexity in the payment methodologies which nobody understands, but helps to create lucrative health insurance companies, which now rival the National Rifle Association in lobbying power.

The result of the additional $70-plus million given by Congress in the first half of 2017 has been to focus the debate around insurance policies, as if that was the core of reform needed. We have watched our professional physician organizations be emasculated by the movement toward salaried positions controlled by payor contracts.

In other words, your doctor likely now works for your insurer rather than for you.

We have watched our family physicians retire early, or be forced to join a "group" to escape financial ruin in their solo practice.

We have seen geriatricians almost disappear off the face of the earth, just when we need them the most. We have watched physicians grow increasingly disenchanted with the practice of medicine, spend less time with us than we need, retire early, or simply spend the time we have with them grumbling.

What we haven't done is present physicians, and patients, with an alternative delivery system that will solve the essential problem in American healthcare: It costs too much.

CHAPTER 18

One pill from each bottle

"Ordering expensive tests has become the workaround."

THE FIRST TIME MY PRACTICE WAS FEATURED on NBC's *Today*, I talked about the case of a delightful new couple I had cared for the prior week. Mr. H was 90 and a veteran of World War I.

Mrs. H proudly said she was 89, but I happened to know that she was actually 94. He was younger but blind, and she was somewhat daft but committed to their loving relationship of almost 70 years.

She had been told by their family physician on an office visit to give her blind husband "one pill out of each of his prescription bottles every morning."

I was called the next week by Mrs. H, who told me her husband was "too weak to get out of bed... and he never stays in bed," she said.

The experienced house call doctor recognizes this as a life-threatening complaint for a nonagenarian, so I hurried over to find him pulseless, lying peacefully in bed. By the bed-stand were three pill bottles neatly in a row, all containing the same 40 mg pills of furosemide, a potent diuretic.

Being blind, Mr. H had been dutifully following his dutiful wife's instruction to "take one pill from each bottle" each morning, giving him a triple dose of a major diuretic for over a week. There is virtually no way I could ever have sorted this out from the perspective of an office or ER visit. The regimen had almost killed him.

Without asking Mr. H to sit up, get in a car, or go to the emergency room, any one of which could have caused a stroke in a 90-year-old with no blood pressure, I quickly put in an intravenous line to rehydrate him in his bedroom, drawing a small amount at the same time for analysis on my portable iSTAT lab instrument.

This is the same treatment we teach in ER residencies, and takes about five minutes to begin. Each liter of Ringer's Lactated fluid cost me $1.57, while a hospital will charge as much as $600 for the same liter of fluid.

About the size of an old telephone handset, the iSTAT allowed me to put one drop of blood on an electronic cartridge, push it in my federally-licensed lab machine, and in two minutes get the results for the following measurements:

- Electrolytes, including sodium, potassium, chloride and bicarbinate
- Hemoglobin, indicating anemia or whether someone has been bleeding
- Glucose, to assess nutritional status and diabetes
- Bun, to assess the state of dehydration and kidney function
- pH, to assess the critical acid-base balance in the body
- PCO2, to assess the adequacy of breathing in patients who are short of breath
- Anion gap, used to assess renal function and electrolyte disturbances
- Base deficit, used to assess the level of shock or acid-base imbalance (for many things that can go wrong)

Whether in an ER or your bedroom, this panel of tests is just about all we need for emergencies. In the ER, it is usually billed out at more than $2,000.

In my patient's bedroom, for the cost of a $6.50 iSTAT cartridge and a few minutes of my time, I was able to determine Mr. H's blood chemistry results.

He had the usual electrolyte abnormalities we see in overdoses of diuretics like furosemide (low sodium and potassium), but his BUN was so high I had to use an additional $6.50 cartridge for creatinine measurement to make sure his kidneys weren't failing.

They weren't, and his strong heart allowed for aggressive rehydration with fluids containing lots of salt and potassium over the next 24 hours to return him to his normal, ambulatory self.

Sitting by the bedside the first couple of hours to monitor his heart's response to hydration, I listened to Mr. H tell me about the worst problem they had on the Maginot Line: "the rats."

He said they were everywhere, so they had to put their food packs inside their shirts to keep the rats from eating them. The real problem came when he fell asleep. That's when the rats would tear into his shirt, often biting him in the process and waking him up.

I had been taught it was trench foot that most bedeviled WWI troops. But it was rats. Nearly 80 years later, even in his blindness, Mr. H told me he still felt those rats.

———

What a privilege it was to meet and treat a hero of World War I.

Administering fluids and other simple procedures in the home requires a physician to slow down and take a full history, if not smell the roses. A quick call to his loving family prevented Mr. and Mrs. H from becoming too independent on their own in the future.

One of his local sons, eligible for Medicare himself, said he would drop by every day to check on them and the medications, which he did for a few more years until Mr. H peacefully passed away.

———

Our population is aging rapidly, with all the WWI veterans now gone and hundreds of WWII veterans dying every day.

Likewise, over 10,000 Americans are newly-qualified for Medicare each day, and the over-80 age group is the fastest-growing decile in our population. It was not uncommon for me to complete a day of house calls when all the patients are nonagenarians or centenarians.

The most prevalent characteristic of this aging/aged population is their subtle deterioration in memory and, hence, the ability to give an accurate history. I don't think I ever had a day of house calls in which something dramatic wasn't discovered in the patient's home, which changed entirely my initial impression of their original complaint.

In addition to the average 45-minute appointments doctors spend with each house call patient simply listening, we are looking around, actively searching for cues to minimize their risks, cue their memories for key items, trying to locate all the pill bottles in their cabinets and drawers, often making observations to establish social bonds without which a treatment plan is often ignored.

Sometimes, it was useful to simply wait for the patient to tell me what was wrong with them. Almost every sick patient will describe a bonafide medical syndrome – that is, if you just wait long enough.

In the ER, with an average face-to-face time of three minutes being standard today, there is no such time for a good history, so ordering expensive tests has become the workaround.

As we all know, such tests can lead to more tests and complications.

CHAPTER 19

My father and the hero

*"It was almost two years after Fallujah,
and something was wrong."*

MY FATHER WAS SHORT ON WORDS AT HOME, a trait I wish I had inherited.

For one thing, he was rarely home, but that gave his words even greater stature when he was. My sister and I tend to recall the same poignant bromides he used to repeat.

One of these was, "Find something you are passionate about, and then become an expert in it."

So, that became my story.

I was privileged to follow some very big shoes, and perhaps lucky to be afflicted with a huge dose of ADHD that only became sublimated when I started making house calls.

It was literally the only thing since college I have done for more than three years. I never would have found my way without discovering the intimacy of patient's homes, and the lessons they taught me.

My father was one of those rare individuals you could know well, yet never know which side he was on, especially when it came to politics. His entire life was more devoted to bringing people together, not apart.

He once received death threats before an interview on CNN about the need for a Palestinian homeland long before it became a reality.

He founded the International Bahraini-American Friendship Society a generation before the 9/11 attacks made it obvious that we should learn more about our Arab brothers.

Sent to Washington to become President of the National War College, he retired as the first President of the National Defense University, having changed the name and combined the War College with the Industrial College of the Armed Forces.

"It's not about war," he often said. "It should be about peace."

—⟁—

Growing up, we were a Navy family, through and through.

Born into blue-and-gold diapers, I watched my father transition from his WWII submarines to become project officer for the top-secret mission in 1958 taking the *USS Nautilus*, our first nuclear sub, under the North Pole.

Only my father, along with Captain William R. Anderson of *Nautilus*, Admiral Arleigh Burke as Chief of Naval Operations, and President Eisenhower knew about the mission.

Even Admiral Rickover, the "Father of the Nuclear Navy" who built the *Nautilus*, wasn't told of the risky Arctic mission.

My father was Special Assistant to the Secretary of the Navy (Fred Korth), yet he couldn't even tell his boss, who was a member of Nixon's Cabinet. When Admiral Burke and Dad gave their last briefing to the President, Eisenhower said something like:

"Well, good luck, gentlemen. Of course, if something happens, we never had this conversation."

That could have been the beginning of presidential "plausible deniability."

Dad later went on to become Commander of all NATO submarines in the Mediterranean Sea. He served as the first Commander of the Middle Force – a role made famous by General Norman Schwartzkopf during the two Iraq wars – then the first president of the National Defense University as a Presidential appointee.

Through it all, my father had the ability to turn every controversy into a discussion about helping each other.

For example, the same day Supreme Court justice Harry Blackmun gave the keynote address at Dad's retirement ceremony in 1977, my father drove his 12-year-old clunker to rural Virginia and began a second career as the best friend of a black crab fisherman. They built outhouses for the indigent and re-roofed trailer homes.

A year earlier, this highly educated, but relatively unknown white Navy Admiral and the black fisherman with a ninth-grade education even convinced two segregated congregations in a rural Virginian town to worship in each other's church ... once.

It was a beginning.

Yet, it was only at his gravesite that I became aware of his power in bringing people together. Perhaps it was seeing his own father dying of tuberculosis when he was 8 years old that made him so independent-minded.

Perhaps it was being named "Marmaduke" that made him an over-achiever, long before the song "A Boy Named Sue" became a hit.

Whatever it was, and whatever job he held during his 32-year Naval career and a generation in retirement, he always seemed to leave reconciliation in his wake.

In 2005, I found myself sitting at an open grave in Arlington National Cemetery, crying softly while the Marines folded his flag. Behind me, leaning on his cane, was Sergeant Oscar Cannon, the Hero of Fallujah, the 2004 battle in which 51 U.S. troops were killed and hundreds wounded seriously. Iraqi losses were estimated at 1,200 or more.

He was in his Marine "dress blues" uniform for the first time since taking seven rounds through his torso and being blown 30 feet in the air by a rocket-propelled grenade.

After he came out of a month-long coma, you may recall footage of President George W. Bush openly weeping at his bedside while he pinned the Silver Star on one of his bandages.

Oscar had come to my father's funeral at my invitation.

I had met Oscar after an urgent phone call from the CEO of a large public company based in New York. I didn't know the CEO, but he knew I was a former Navy doctor, and that his protégé, Oscar Cannon, had just called him from San Diego's Naval Hospital after the 81st operation to save his left leg.

It was almost two years after Fallujah, and something was wrong. The CEO asked if I would go see what was wrong with Oscar's medical care.

"I have a private jet standing by," he said. "You take Oscar to the best hospital in the country and get the best doctors. Cost is no object."

When I met Oscar lying in the ICU, he was tied to monitors by the usual array of tubes and wires. The thing that struck me most was his primary concern for his fellow Marines, and his lack of concern for his own situation. The grenade had blown his left leg apart over a year before.

The bone shards were still being held together by external bolts and gears, the exposed muscles covered in dressings after yet another attempt to create enough blood supply for the leg to heal.

Oscar had refused to let them amputate. Hence, the prolonged recovery during a year of multiple operations by vascular and orthopedic surgeons on both Coasts trying innovative methods to save his leg.

"No, no, don't worry about me," he insisted. "I already have the best surgeons and medical care I could hope for. I was only concerned about the guy in the bed next to me back at Walter Reed Hospital in Washington. For six weeks, he has been lying there with no arms and bandages over both eyes. I think he's blind.

"Nobody but doctors and nurses have come to see him since he's been in the hospital."

Oscar's concern was heartfelt and genuine.

"You know, doctor," Oscar continued, "we are just kids. The first thing that happens to you when you get injured is that you lose combat pay."

I sat in stunned silence.

"We're getting the best medical care in the world, I am sure, but we don't have the skills to navigate our social problems from a hospital bed."

I asked him what sort of social problems he was he talking about.

"In my case, combat pay was the difference between my new wife being able to fly to Walter Reed from Camp Pendleton to visit me last year."

He said the only time she visited she vomited after watching them change his leg dressings.

He kept repeating, "We're just kids, you know. They tell me to get a civilian lawyer for my divorce, but I don't know how to do that, and I don't have any money to afford one. I thought the JAG officers could handle it, but for some reason they can't."

Quickly, Oscar changed the subject back to another of his fellow inmates, this time at the Navy hospital in San Diego.

"They flew me out here from Walter Reed for special surgery," he said, "but there's a guy here with no legs that has been sobbing constantly since I arrived. Nobody has come to console him, counsel him, or even befriend him. That's not right."

He continued, "I am so lucky to have a rich mentor in New York, but many of these kids don't have any family to help them through this. All we really want to do is wear our uniform again and get back to our units to do our job, but you need social, not just medical, support to handle the issues we face … and we're just kids."

There it was again.

Oscar's self-effacing concern for his fellow soldiers kept surfacing during the hour-long visit I was privileged to spend with him. I told him that I knew that there was always a doctor with the rank of Rear Admiral assigned the title of Medical Officer to the Marines. That was the person who needed to hear his story.

I told him I didn't know who that was, but that I would find out and promised that either I, or someone my father knew back in Washington would exert some pressure to see what could be done.

After that, I immediately went back to running my venture capital-backed house call company … and promptly forgot about Oscar. I'm not proud of this, and there are no excuses to be made. Life continually gives us opportunity for reconciliation, but we are too scared or too busy to respond.

It was months after I met Oscar that I received word that my father's remains would be placed in the ground at Arlington National Cemetery with what is called "Full Military Honors."

Dad had finally passed away after winning the fight with six of his seven different cancers during the past 30 years.

I had kept in contact with Oscar but produced nothing of value for him or his Marines. My excuse was telling myself that my practice was in San Diego, and Oscar had been returned to Walter Reed for rehabilitation of his leg in Washington D.C.

For some reason, perhaps repressed guilt at having lost touch with him, I reached out to Oscar and asked if he would do our family the honor of attending my Dad's funeral.

He seemed delighted, and said he had been looking for an opportunity to "wear my dress blues" for some time. Dad's funeral would be the occasion.

We decided to meet at the graveside, since Oscar still could not endure the long walk down the hill behind the horse-drawn caisson. Full military honors for a Vice Admiral means six horses, a marching band, and a 17-gun salute, the blasts fading slowly as you walk down the long, sloping path to an open grave.

The honors also mandate that a flag officer (Rear Admiral or above) deliver the folded flag to any flag-officer's widow.

As a Navy Rear Admiral in his full-dress white uniform bent over my Mother, saying the words of tribute that begin with "On behalf of a grateful nation…," I barely could control myself.

I knew the sacrifices my father had made for his country over the years, from being depth-charged in his submarine in WWII to the many years at sea, to the week he spent sleeping on a cot next to Robert Kennedy during the Cuban Missile Crisis, and during his time as Commander of the Middle East Force.

I was also thinking about Oscar's sacrifice as he stood behind us in his magnificent Marine Dress Blue uniform, leaning on his cane and crippled for life.

These are the people who fight for us and don't care which side of the political spectrum we believe. We tend to just think of them as warriors, when all other options for a peaceful community have failed.

Just when the service was about to start, the Navy Admiral in charge of my Dad's funeral quietly took a seat next to my wife, who was seated next to me. In the formality of the moment, I didn't recognize him until I heard his voice.

"When I saw the name 'Marmaduke,' I knew this must be your father-in-law," he whispered to my wife. "I was in surgical residency with your husband and came today to honor your family."

I suddenly recognized the voice of an orthopedic surgeon I had spent some time training with back in San Diego. After the ceremony was completed, I composed myself and approached the Admiral, who was patiently waiting off to the side.

"Tom, you were so great to come on this special occasion; my eternal thanks," I said. "By the way, what are you doing now? I didn't even know you had made Admiral!"

Tom said he had just been promoted and recently relocated to Washington D.C. One of his duties on Saturdays was either to make rounds at Walter Reed Hospital or present the flag to the widows of other flag officers at Arlington National Cemetery. He had recognized my Father's name, so decided to come here for us.

"That is just fantastic, Tom, and thanks again," I blurted. "But what is your job now in Washington?"

"I've just been assigned as the Medical Officer to the Marines," he said.

I asked him if he had a few minutes to meet someone special. Oscar limped over with his cane, then suddenly became erect and saluted as only a Marine in dress blues can.

"Sergeant Oscar Cannon, United States Marine Corps, sir. Pleased to meet you, Admiral."

Tom smiled as he returned Oscar's salute.

"I know who you are, Oscar. I operated on your leg once."

Six months later, the first Wounded Warriors program, created to meet the social needs of our injured veterans, opened at Walter Reed and San Diego Naval Hospital.

Postscript: After returning to Iraq as an instructor for one tour and becoming a public figure as a Wounded Warriors spokesperson, Staff Sgt Oscar Cannon died from complications of his wounds in 2012. He was 29.

CHAPTER 20

A matter of Faith

"I don't ever want my neighbors seeing me leave my house feet first."

AT 83, FAITH KLEVEN REMAINED an extraordinary woman. Afflicted with rheumatic heart disease as a young girl, she had received one of the first artificial heart valves.

Later, on the way to her wedding, a drunk driver had crippled her for life. Despite a pair of legs the size of chopsticks, she remained active, mostly by constantly doing things for other people.

What you had to understand about Faith Kleven was her constant need to keep moving. Perhaps being told she would never walk again so many times as a young woman motivated her.

With her beautific smile, rapid speech pattern, and "never enough hours in the day" personality, expecting Faith to rest in bed the afternoon after her cardiac catheterization had been unrealistic.

So there I was on Friday night, the neighborhood doctor holding a compression bandage over a leaking artery left by the new cardiologist that morning. The heart catheter study had been ominous, so her cardiologist had joined her lung specialist and recommended hospice, the program for patients with less than six months to live.

I looked at the amount of blood covering her bed.

It was comforting to know I could measure the blood she had lost using the portable lab instrument tucked away in my black bag.

However, it was both cheaper and quicker to glance at her bedsheets, yet another cost-effective advantage of making house calls.

Holding a compression bandage for an hour over a bleeding artery in someone's bedroom also offers a great opportunity to take the kind of history we are too busy to entertain in a normal office practice, let alone the busy ER.

In my emergency room, with numerous sick patients needing urgent help, I doubt she would have received much of my attention for this rather simple problem.

Now, aware that the "community standard of care" for an arterial bleed would be to send her to the emergency room, I was poised to listen carefully to Faith, as she described her increasing shortness of breath over the past few months.

After a while, I picked up on historical clues to an obscure disease called pulmonary interstitial fibrosis (PIF), with symptoms similar to her congestive heart failure, the condition her doctors were treating. In the emergency room, I would have been distracted getting redundant blood tests she didn't need, as well as another chest X-ray to track her heart failure.

Once the bleeding stopped in the ER, I would have discharged her and sent her back to the cardiologist, forgetting entirely about her, and certainly missing out on what became a much-valued relationship.

Weeks after an ER visit, she would have received a Medicare "Explanation of Benefits" stating that Medicare would pay 80% of the allowed $2,800 out of an ER bill for over $12,000. In her bedroom, my extended history cost nothing but a little time, and ultimately saved her life, all for less than $150.

The day after my hour-long hand pressure finally stopped her bleeding artery, I enrolled her in an experimental telemonitoring project funded personally by Dr. Patrick Soon-Shiong.

—◦◦◦—

Dr. Soon-Shiong is a modern-day da Vinci, having committed both his genius and his billions to fix the myriad of issues related to sharing secure patient information between patients and multiple healthcare providers.

He had recently hired me to help develop his home-care program, and we chose Faith as the first of 22 of my most complex, home-bound patients to receive his new "plug and play" telemonitor – so simple to use that "even a doctor could install it."

On the way to the airport the next day, I plugged this HBox monitor into Faith's home, put a new wireless, wearable oximeter on her, attached a pulse and activity monitor to her clothing … and raced off to the airport to give a talk in Dallas.

What occurred during my flight that day in 2012 was, most likely, the first time any doctor has had the privilege of making the real-time diagnosis of a complex medical issue based on remote telemonitoring during a commercial flight.

The wireless sensors Faith now wore sent signals to the HBox that was plugged into her wall receptacle, which then automatically uploaded her data continuously to the Internet. From there, the data streamed through a secure website to be instantly graphed by special software that I could remotely program to alert me by text, email, or automated cellphone contact.

Being a passenger that day on one of the first Southwest Airlines flights equipped with WiFi, I logged into the Nant Health website to see how Faith was doing … and was amazed.

There, clear as day, was the reason Faith was short of breath. It was not early pneumonia, bronchitis, a pulmonary embolism or her worsening congestive heart failure, any of which could have explained her worsening shortness of breath.

Watching Faith's pulse and oxygen levels chart across the screen at the same time her activity monitor recorded her steps, I could see the sudden, profound drop in oxygen levels characteristic of PIF.

Nothing but PIF drops oxygen levels so fast and so far with such little activity. It meant Faith was being over-treated for heart failure, making her weak and causing risky changes in her electrolytes, when PIF was the culprit.

As soon as I got off the plane, I called Faith and told her to stop the high-dose diuretic that was making her so weak. I told her that I would see her and explain things when I got back the next day. Never before have doctors had such powerful tools to extend their cognitive services in real time, rather than wait for the patient to come to the office for a scheduled visit.

By "virtualizing" the care of complex patients, we can not only enter their homes for a scheduled (or urgent) housecall, we can be there virtually all the time with powerful new sensors that tell us the key physiologic parameters that separate the emergencies from the routine.

Such is the hidden value of house call medicine: while creating a massive disruption in healthcare referral patterns, what Faith wanted in the first place was a disposition from the privacy of her own home. As one elderly patient once told me: "Not only are sirens annoying, I don't ever want my neighbors seeing me leave my house feet first."

While upsetting to the ambulance industry and the emergency department money machine, which typically admits 25% of ER patients to the hospital, an urgent housecall usually allows a patient to be stabilized at home, avoiding the ambulance ride, costly ER bill, and exposure to the "bad bugs" hiding in hospitals, as well as reducing the risk of preventable hospital readmissions.

Due to a genetic abnormality in Faith's clotting mechanism, it took almost an hour to stop her bleeding, but it was an hour well spent. As I listened to this remarkable woman's medical saga, she told me she that despite her increasing shortness of breath, nothing her cardiologist or pulmonologist did seemed to help.

As her catheter site finally stopped bleeding, Faith told her doctors she had refused the hospice referral. Clearly, she wasn't ready to give up.

Even tied to the green oxygen tubing trailing behind her throughout the house, Faith continued to remain active. Her doctors didn't have the benefit of seeing her behavior at home. Faith didn't just get up from a chair. She jumped up from her chair and charged across the room, usually to do something for someone else.

Indeed, every house call I ever made for her was interrupted by numerous phone calls from friends she had helped in some way.

I soon realized I was being introduced to yet another very special life worth living to its fullest. Rarely in the average time of three to eight minutes that ER doctors spend with their patients, have I had time to develop such important insight into my patients' lives.

Faith was like so many high-cost patients consuming 80% of the U.S. healthcare resources, despite constituting only 8% of our population. She was medically complicated with multiple chronic diseases. She had major infirmities limiting her Activities of Daily Living (ADLs).

Things like bathing or even going to the bathroom had risks: of falling, of disconnecting her oxygen, of becoming so short of breath with the exertion she had another heart attack.

Perhaps most indicative of her future high costs to the standard American healthcare system, she had already had multiple recent, urgent hospitalizations for heart failure and pneumonia.

An elderly patient like Faith with five chronic conditions is nearly 100 times as likely to be admitted to the hospital for a preventable condition in the next year. They average over $75,000 in Medicare payments during the next year.

The expense will occur mostly in hospitals and emergency rooms, during home health and hospice periods, or in a skilled nursing facility for those who "need institutionalization," a disturbing term in and of itself.

None of these venues are desired by our patients, yet they clamor for the lowly house call. What could be professionally more rewarding for a physician than responding to the desire of the Greatest Generation while showing the way to a cure for Medicare's feared insolvency?

The 32 office-based Demonstration Projects funded through Obamacare's Medicare Innovation Center cost over $30 billion, yet provided no savings. The reasons cited by the Congressional Budget Office and reported in *The New England Journal of Medicine* are two.

First, provisions of new services like 24-hour nurse Call Centers increased access and improved patient satisfaction, but the "woodwork effect" attracted new patients who normally would not have tried to penetrate the modern maze of services. This form of increased access created new costs for the system.

Secondly, when sick patients are calling to present their urgent problems to their assigned healthcare "provider," the provider incurs a legal and ethical obligation to consider the worst-case scenario.

Hence, potentially sick patients are often referred by phone to the emergency room, where costs escalate quickly with the added ambulance rides and hospitalizations.

Well-meaning nurses on Call Center phones must tell patients to schedule an appointment they often don't need, since they cannot practice medicine; office doctors triage patients to the emergency room after hours for their own convenience and protection, with the homebound patient in a wheelchair usually needing a $1,200 ambulance ride just to get "checked out."

However, when a primary care physician has an option to use the inexpensive, urgent house call supported with modern testing equipment, patient calls for information can be met with a cost-effective solution that is both safe and patient-friendly.

—◦◦◦—

The passion that I have in my soul for house calls never wavered after some 40 years. Yet, for many of those years, I wasn't smart enough to recognize all the treasure created by a mobile practice.

Just by hanging out the "I make house calls" sign, any doctor soon aggregates the very high-cost tranche of patients the insurance industry has trouble identifying.

They are the ones who call us and drop their personal doctor of 40 years the first time we come to their home in a time of need.

The pirfenadone prevented progression of Faith's PIF for almost three years. She never returned to an emergency room or the hospital.

The intimacy and trusting relationships developed with her family during the home visits continues to reward me with a deep sense of professional fulfillment.

Indeed, providing comprehensive care to her at home had been A Matter of Faith.

CHAPTER 21

The White House is calling

"Enjoying the moment, with more than a bit of pomposity."

A FEW WEEKS AFTER President George Herbert Walker Bush's emergency aero-vac to Bethesda Naval Hospital, I was sitting at a large, round table with six hospital executives in Eagle Pass, Texas, a remote city on the fringes of society where they mostly make their own rules.

We were discussing the option of building a heliport for an air ambulance at their tiny hospital with limited resources. My role in the group was that of Chief Medical Officer to Critical Air Medicine, a national air ambulance company that provided transports for critical patients from rural sites to major trauma centers.

Air ambulance transports are so lucrative the company could offer to build the hospital their own heliport outside the ER and staff the helicopter team with pilots and flight nurses to cover 24/7, all at no cost to the hospital.

A waitress came to the table and loudly asked: "Is one of you Dr. Bayne? The White House is calling you."

Everyone at the table looked stunned. You could hear a pin drop.

This is about as good as it gets for anyone in a consulting position.

Enjoying the moment, with more than a bit of pomposity, I asked the waitress: "Please ask who at the White House is calling."

The waitress looked confused, but quickly came back with: "They say the President's physician would like to speak with you."

I left the dumbstruck table to take the call.

It was a military doctor on President Reagan's White House staff whom I had helped train in the Navy. He had seen yet another piece about our house call company on the "Today Show" and wondered if I would be willing to consult with the White House to bring Air Force One up to our standards for house calls.

Of course, the answer was yes, and I soon found out that the medical supplies for the most powerful person in the world on Air Force One were barely rudimentary.

Today, the President's physicians have upgraded Air Force One and their carry-bags to include the use of oximeters, portable lab instruments, and various other technologies we had found useful during our home visits.

—⋙⋘—

That foray into Washington's inside track should have made the house call movement easier, but it didn't.

In 1989, Congress had mandated that physicians should be paid fair value for their work and practice expenses. The new law outlined over 7,000 specific physician services, which were each given a five-digit "CPT code" for billing purposes. A multi-year study was then done to determine the reasonable fee associated with each code.

Only one type of physician encounter was left out of the study: home visits.

Using the rationale that "doctors don't make house calls anymore," federal bureaucrats in 1990 decided to simply guess at a value for the basic house call and came up with $42 as total compensation for a moderately complex, established patient home visit.

For lab and X-rays done at the patient's home, Medicare usually refused payment, citing a code which translated to "not paid for in this setting."

It had never occurred to me that Medicare would simply refuse payment without any attempt to study house calls or comply with their own 1989 law requiring appropriate payment for the "work and practice" expenses of providing these services.

I knew I was avoiding at least one hospital admission (averaging over $10,000 in 1989) every day I made my average of seven home visits. That's exactly what happened, though. Even when I did charge this nominal amount of $42, I was often denied payment for spurious reasons.

Back in the mid-1980s, the American Academy of Home Care Physicians had even persuaded several Congress members to sponsor a lawsuit against the federal government under what is called a write of mandamus.

The lawsuit resulted in a federal court ruling that required Medicare to obey the law and pay for home visits when they were deemed "medically reasonable and necessary."

The most vexing issue for Medicare auditors was repetitive, daily visits. Prior to the lawsuit, if a physician billed for three consecutive daily house calls, the third visit was denied under a rationale that "the patient should be hospitalized."

It was as if the hospital was a disease category and you simply couldn't be that sick at home.

No other type of physician service has ever been subjected to such convoluted logic as physician home visits. After following one bureaucrat's recommendation to submit an application for a research grant to prove my assumptions of the house call program, all three Medicare reviewers rejected our grant proposal for the same reason.

One wrote: "This type of service is not feasible," despite the fact we had been doing it for over ten years, were financed by some of the most prestigious investment bankers in America, and had expanded to eleven cities in five states.

Meanwhile, all our lab tests and x-rays were still being routinely denied in the mid-'90s because "this service is not feasible in this setting." Our 1991 grant proposal was essentially the same one now called the "Independence at Home Medicare Demonstration."

Fortunately, at the same time the government had denied us payment, there were some brave venture capitalists who believed in house calls as a viable life-saving and cost-effective way to practice medicine.

They had funded our company, which gave me the privilege of being able to provide the best and most appropriate care, including that which is necessary to rule out true emergencies and/or definitively treat patients at home.

I will be forever indebted to them for committing over $30 million in capital to support our efforts to demonstrate the value of the lowly house call in health-care reform.

They lost it all, but we didn't lose the war. Not yet anyway.

PART 5

A better mouse-trap

CHAPTER 22

Your heart simply goes out

"Her family wishes for her to be comfortable."

THERE SHE WAS, JUST AS I LEFT HER, curled up on her right side asleep in the same Velcro'd pants doubling as pajamas, suspiciously bulky around her shrunken buttocks.

Has she been incontinent? Her dementia is advanced now, the drugs no longer working, or did they ever? Should I stop them?

She is my mother and she is resting comfortably in her room in a convalescent home, where the quality of care is high but the outlook for recovery is extremely low. More likely, zero.

If I happen to see conditions or procedures or treatments that aren't quite right, what are the rules for interfering with her daily care? Should I use my rank to make something better happen? What does "better" even mean?

I am her son.

Should I wake her?

The position she is in cannot be good for her spinal stenosis. Is the Naprosyn still working? When I ask my mother if she's in any pain, she shakes her head. She's always been that way, rarely outwardly complaining.

She tries to speak, with stories that seem to be dangling on the tip of her tongue.

Like the one about the damn dog, when my mother and I paid an "assisted-living" visit to Dad late in his shortened life.

Dad clumsily got out of bed to greet us, but got tangled up in the dog's leash and fell down on top of the adored family pet.

At that, my mother, much more concerned about the dog's well-being, snapped up the little offender and angrily harrumphed out of the room. That left Dad helplessly spread-eagled on the floor, his bare rump glistening with the ever-present cleft of a nightgown that never fully covers.

That's when I realized she was almost gone.

———⟋⟍⟋———

So this is it?

You mean to tell me that I flew 3,000 miles, rented a car, drove three hours to have a conversation she'll never remember? I decide to sit on the sofa and read a magazine, letting her sleep.

Time passes slowly. I have placed framed photos of her great-grandchildren – my grandchildren – a reassuring visual treat for her, I'm hoping. Yet I don't know if she'll even recognize them, and right now she's in a deep sleep and I don't want to wake her up.

Sitting there, frustrated at this disease I cannot master, I remember what I had told my father years ago: "There will be times when it is virtually impossible to see her as just sick, rather than incredibly selfish."

That was years ago.

———⟋⟍⟋———

My mother remains in a vegetative state in a Virginia nursing home, age 98 and holding.

She was blessed with a strong heart, but cursed with the genetics of a form of dementia we still don't understand very well. The only time she has been to the hospital in the past decade of her coma was when she fell out of bed and broke her arm.

Her doctor makes periodic house calls and sees her every month or so, just to check on her medications. He knows that her family, including me, wishes for her to be comfortable, and expects nothing more.

As her son, I realize there's not much else anyone can do except allowing her final days, weeks, months or perhaps years take their natural course.

As it has been for 30 years, I know that's all I can do.

CHAPTER 23

Left with the warm fuzzies

"Carrying a blood sample back to the hospital lab imposes all sorts of error-potential."

MORE THAN A FEW YEARS AGO, I was sitting around yet another table with a group of nationally-known medical leaders, again being the only person in the room I had never heard of.

The head of Medicaid was asking us why we liked making home visits.

The future President of the American Academy of Home Care Medicine said with the accustomed high praise: "I can't tell you how rewarding it is. Yesterday, I saw a patient with multiple problems, including the possibility of internal bleeding. I was able to draw the blood at home and take it back to the hospital to test for anemia, a test this homebound patient never would have gotten without a trip to the emergency room."

All heads nodded in affirmation, except mine.

Instead, I was cringing with embarrassment. This was exactly the problem we had to correct in mainstream medicine: The misguided thinking that the status quo was OK as long as small, incremental improvements might be made.

In my world of emergency medicine, it is incomprehensible to think of leaving a patient's home who might be bleeding to death internally without knowing they are not. Carrying a blood sample back to the hospital lab imposes all sorts of error-potential, not the least of which is they could bleed to death before the sample is measured.

The blood-carrying doctor could be distracted by another urgent call. The sample could bake in the sun on the back seat of her car. It could get lost, forgotten, corrupted or stolen. She could have a car accident on the way back to the lab.

The patient thinks of none of these possibilities.

Instead, they are left with the warm fuzzies of thinking any doctor nice enough to visit their home surely wouldn't let such an important test be delayed or forgotten.

What I have learned is that it's most important to inform such patients what we are not able to do, rather than bask in the low-hanging fruit of beating the office competition. For instance, I make a point of telling patients now that I am actually retired and they cannot expect to get me on the phone.

When actively making 7 to 10 house calls daily over the years, I learned to tell patients my "ground rules" on the first visit:

- I generally don't make house calls after 6 pm or on week-ends
- I also try to take a vacation on rare occasions; if so, there will be another doctor or physician assistant available to you
- In urgent situations, you cannot always expect to get me, but you will get someone within the hour
- I cannot control what happens once we have to call 9-1-1 unless I ride in the ambulance with you
- I can only control which hospital we admit you to if we don't call 9-1-1, which is usually possible, since I carried all the emergency stabilization testing and equipment the paramedics did
- State law now prevents me from getting malpractice insurance to set bone fractures, but I will stabilize any fracture and refer you directly to an orthopedist to bypass the ER
- State pharmacy regulations have now made it impossible for me to carry the 95 different pre-packaged prescriptions I used

to carry to treat any, and every, urgency likely to need medications, but still carry the important ones

- New federal regulations now make it so onerous that carrying intravenous opiates is also problematic, so don't tell anyone I do (under my personal DEA license)

In short, I learned the hard way to disavow the patient of what I called "The Great White Knight Syndrome." Even then, I knew I was usually leaving the patient with a feeling of such relief that heightened expectations were to be expected.

When the patient sees such a better mousetrap, it is only reasonable for them to expect their house to be mouse-free from then on.

Trouble is, it isn't.

CHAPTER 24

The devil lurks

*"The aging of America continues to drive the
increased number of heart attacks and strokes."*

A U.S. GOVERNMENT STUDY IN 2013 analyzed some 22,000 paramedic injuries sustained in ambulance transports during a five-year period.

There were 59 fatalities, mostly from traffic accidents while careening around town despite sirens blaring and lights flashing. The paramedic injury rate was three times that of national occupational risk profiles, with women representing 29% of the workforce, yet sustaining 47% of the injuries.

It is clear that unrestrained occupants trying to save our lives in the back of speeding ambulances are at high risk for fatal injuries themselves during collisions. The risk of assault by drug-addled patients is also not insignificant.

Patients who are restrained recumbent in the back of an ambulance are much less likely to be injured, but little attempt to study the risk for patients has occurred.

Of even more interest is the fact that data on whether the patients involved in fatal accidents were actually critically ill has never been published.

We hear little about the risk to paramedics on the job, preferring to be kept in the dark so the highly-inefficient and lucrative ambulance industry can continue to grow.

A Life Flight crash taught me that the devil lurks in hidden details often ignored in our enthusiasm to catch up to the advanced systems developed by the military.

Although we can thank the Civil War for the invention of ground ambulance transportation, the Korean Conflict for bringing surgical care closer to the field by MASH units, and Vietnam for the maturation of helicopter-based aeromedical rescues, our civilian risk/benefit analysis is distinctly different.

I believe the dot-com communications revolution has provided us with such technologies that a complete review of prehospital care delivery is needed. When a paramedic under your physician's telephonic/virtual supervision can perform iSTAT blood tests, organize portable X-rays, and perform many minor procedures, a new opportunity for pre-hospital care opens up.

The aging of America continues to drive the increased number of heart attacks and strokes that fuel the growth in ambulance rides, yet virtually no organized attempt to coordinate EMS with the primary care of geriatricians is underway.

Currently, the closest thing we have is the movement to gentrify, or "geriatrify" American emergency rooms, making them more hospital to the elderly. Piping in soft music and painting the walls mauve will not save lives. At best, it is foolhardy to think such cosmetics are necessary in true emergencies.

With government regulation of payment methodologies, the $8 billion U.S. ambulance industry has been forced to change significantly in the past few years. Medicare, Medicaid and other government programs are responsible for almost two-thirds of ambulance transportation payments, and the aging demographics seem to mandate unbridled growth.

I believe it should be reduced, and markedly so, given the data on elderly ER usage.

In a four-year phase-in of new Medicare payment methodologies, no longer are ambulance transports paid without questions asked. Today, you should expect payment for your ambulance ride only when "another form of transportation would have reasonably been expected to cause harm to the patient."

This pre-supposes an advanced knowledge of medical risks in a vast number of emergency conditions, and puts the patient at risk for self-rationing when it might cost them their life.

In response, some innovative paramedic programs are changing the model from "scoop and haul" to "catch and release."

Under various state law exemptions, paramedics can put elderly seniors back into the bed from which they fell without transporting them to the ER. This makes intuitive sense, especially since a one-way transport by ambulance cost over $1,000 in most major cities of America.

However, as a former director of both civilian and military EMS systems, I would point out that ER physicians may not be the best specialists to design a new delivery model.

This fact should give us pause: Two-thirds of over 3,000 new patients would rather have called a mobile doctor they don't know for a service they have never seen than calling 9-1-1.

It suggests to me that the ambulance industry might well think of what the patient needs, rather than what they get paid to deliver.

Even more disturbing was the 22% of patients who said they would have done "nothing" without the first home visit. We had an internist review their charts and opine on their treatment. Fully 20% of the "nothings" qualified for emergency admission to the hospital, to which they were referred.

In our above survey, 22% of patients said they would have done "nothing" without the first home visit.

Yet, only half of them went!

The other half said they would rather wait for us to come back tomorrow and re-evaluate them.

The real need is for acute *and* trend-line information for urgent situations. That information should be offered at the highest level of decision-making – not the lowest.

In other words, a physician-level triage encounter interview should be integrated with any new reform, and that triage must include both ER physician logic, as well as the deep understanding primary care physicians develop with their patients over time.

Modern communication makes this feasible, if not mandatory. The potential savings are immense if a house call is now one of their options.

Over the years, additional options such as paramedic-delivered, onsite triage under virtuous physician supervision and/or definitive care could have replaced the majority of my personal 10,000 house calls.

By thinking of urgent medical situations in two phases, both acute responses and definitive onsite treatments can be driven by what the patients wanted in the first place.

CHAPTER 25

The answer is money

"I was dumbfounded, but it made perfect sense."

THE HEALTH INSURANCE INDUSTRY was quite happy for decades riding the escalating costs.

When I took the chief medical director of Blue Cross of California along with me on my home visits for a day back in the early '90s, I thought my break-through concept was at hand.

The doctor was amazed and quite complimentary at what we could now do in the home—at greatly reduced cost.

When I took him back to his hotel, I asked how to take the concept further so Blue Cross could save money on healthcare payments. He looked confused for a moment, as if deciding whether to tell this naïve doctor how stupid I really was.

"We don't want to save money," he said flatly. "The regulations allow us to base our premiums on a percentage of the cost of care. Obviously, a percentage of a larger number is a larger number."

I was dumbfounded, but it made perfect sense.

In healthcare, the answer is money. And what's the question?

———✺———

The noon meeting came quickly. We had been writing and speaking about terms for continued financing of Call Doctor for several months.

When you receive investor monies, you are obligated to keep them informed of things like cash flow, and ours had run out. With good accounting, it is quite easy to predict the precise day that you will be flat broke.

And now we were.

———⌘———

Of course, our employees didn't know this and neither did the doctors, but telling anyone of the perilous state we were in would've been so destabilizing to the medical group that it had to be kept confidential.

The deal we had discussed for the past two months brought in the sorely-needed new management as well as several million dollars.

I would still have majority ownership of stock, so I didn't worry too much about having the vision changed or corrupted. It was essential to me that true businessmen run this beast, but I also knew the purity of the comprehensive house call concept needed protection for the benefit of future patients.

Instead of a new investment of several million dollars, my investors told me they were going to take over management and commit only to funding our cash flow needs on a month-to-month basis.

It would no longer matter who owned controlling shares in the company if all decisions were under the gun of next month's financial needs.

I had no other option, but something told me that mixing up my vision of comprehensive house calls to the most complex and needy patients in our country with this type of support made no sense.

I don't where the courage came from, but I found myself responding definitively.

"Well, I'm sorry, but this isn't the deal we discussed, and it makes no sense to me," I said.

They left as stunned as I was.

I had no real option other than close Call Doctor down after the last payroll was due by week's end. What my investors didn't know was that I had been making payroll out of my home-equity line of credit for the past six weeks.

I was now out of options.

CHAPTER 26

Great men in medicine

"The problem was, how to invest the $100 million a day in cashflow."

WHEN I BEGAN SURGICAL TRAINING back in the Cenozoic Age, the dinosaurs roaming hospital corridors had names and were accomplishing remarkable things.

Men like Dr. Denton Cooley were inventing heroic operations on the heart and blood vessels while spilling more blood than we had seen since the mutilations of the Civil War.

But when Dr. David Hume, the Father of the kidney transplant, planted himself on the side of a mountain east of San Diego crashing his private plane, it marked the end of an era of Great Men in Medicine.

We don't talk as much about the leaders in surgery or medicine today as we did then. Too bad.

It seems odd that the Information Age is devoid of famous physicians with household names. People like Sir William Osler, the Father of Medicine, or William Halstead, the Father of Surgery, both of the 19th century, don't seem to exist anymore.

Interestingly enough, Halstead died from a delay in gallbladder surgery, and Sir Osler died during the Spanish Flu pandemic with a misdiagnosis. Such were the limitations of "modern medicine" in the 19th century.

Instead of iconic physicians, today's healthcare talent is littered with the household names of big businesses like Blue Cross, United

Healthcare, or the remarkably mis-named Humana Corporation. I suppose it was inevitable that everyone has now heard of United Healthcare, a leviathan with $250 billion in annual revenue. Under the pretext of saving the taxpayer money, the HMO movement has morphed into Big Business.

The "giant sucking sound" you hear is not lost profits from the NAFTA treaty, but the 24% average administrative costs taken out of your monthly premiums before your physician or hospital bills are paid.

If you could name the CEO of United Healthcare, I would be surprised, unless it was the past CEO who became infamous for being the highest paid executive in history with an annual income over $1 billion, mostly from back-dated options now considered illegal.

I was once hired as a "senior medical advisor" by a United Healthcare subsidiary. They paid me $10,000 monthly – and never once called me for two years!

I met him on his way out after the scandal his salary created, leaving United Healthcare in the lurch.

To his credit, he feigned interest in the concept of using house calls to attract the high-cost, homebound patients to a more efficient delivery system. But, alas, the public (plus the SEC), had spoken and he was canned.

One of his successors was introduced to me on a Sunday afternoon at a private residence in San Diego. Ken Burdick, the new CEO of United Healthcare, was appointed to reform the company's image, left in tatters by his uber-wealthy predecessor.

I brought my current version of the black bag, complete with wires coming out of the laptop, a small device showing your EKG when touched to the chest, and the magical iSTAT, a battery-powered, handheld lab instrument that measured everything dispositive in two minutes.

Mr. Burdick was tentatively impressed and asked if I would consider presenting my vision to the monthly Council of Presidents for

United Health Group in Minnesota. This was the break I thought I had been waiting for.

Two months later, my business partner and I signed the register at the security desk outside the huge United Health building and were escorted down what appeared to be a 100-yard empty corridor with pristine surroundings.

Gone were the priceless Greek and Roman statues in the mausoleum which graced the entrance when I presented to the chief operating officer of PacifiCare in 1991.

PacifiCare, now owned by United Health, had asked me to present to their COO, who promptly fell asleep during our brief meeting in Los Angeles. I gently woke him up, so he wouldn't miss the opportunity of a lifetime. But he declined, saying their real problem was not the need for new "gatekeeping" methods of controlling cost.

His biggest challenge, he went on to say, was how to invest to $100 million a *day* in cashflow that kept pouring in. He said they couldn't hire and train the accountants fast enough.

Eventually, PacifiCare offered Call Doctor a one-year contract wherein I would provide a Mobile Physician Treatment Center under their logo and physicians to make house calls for a flat fee of $200. Their plan was to film the MPTC to use when they started their multi-million advertising blitz when introducing their Secure Horizons "product" to San Diego.

It soon became obvious that PacifiCare wanted Call Doctor only to exploit their enrollment potential as they signed up new patients for their HMO. A 30-day contract cancellation clause would have left us unpaid after introduction of an attractive alternative to hundreds of thousands of potential patients.

Years later, I signed a limited trial contract to make urgent house calls to Secure Horizons enrollees when their doctor made the referral. We never got paid, although we saved a few lives for patients whose access to care had been severely restricted by HMO policies.

When it became more widely known that the HMO movement

had failed to save money in population-based studies, Group Health Cooperative of Puget Sound contacted me, resulting in approval for a major new implementation of our urgent house call services.

A picture of the MPTC was published along with a laudatory article about Call Doctor on the front page of the *Seattle Business Journal* to announce the approval of our new house call program by the Group Health Board of Trustees.

Unfortunately, Group Health had recently merged with Kaiser Permanente, and the VP of Marketing overturned the deal.

From a confidential phone call by an insider, I learned the reason for the cancellation was fear that there was no way to control access to a mobile physician service making house calls. Everyone would want the service, which could lead to increased access for the high-cost patients we treated.

This so-called "woodwork effect" has plagued attempts to reduce cost through easy access from Call Center activities under the Obamacare's new name for managed care: "accountable care organizations."

I was unable to convince Group Health marketing executives that we only made house calls to appropriate patients, those who were too sick, too infirm, or too demented to gain access to an office appointment. Even Medicare didn't pay for our services unless it "was medically reasonable and necessary" in the home setting.

Ken Burdick, however, was a different sort of CEO at United Health. He had been brought in to "clean up the public image" of the evil HMO shortly after actress Helen Hunt's famous quote in "As Good As It Gets" made the news: "Fuck the HMO."

Ken truly cared about patients, and he truly wanted to create a system that not only saved societal costs, but provided broad access to all the services that an advanced medical community like San Diego could provide.

As we walked briskly down the long corridor at United Healthcare, I stopped at the one and only attraction on the path. It was a late-model, giant flat screen TV that must have cost $20,000 at the time. It was flashing a chart of data every four seconds, and I just had to see what it was about.

Before the guard noticed I was lagging behind, I figured out that this flashing data was actually the total number of cardiology consults being billed to United Healthcare in the entire country. It was real-time, undoubtedly accurate, and absolutely astounding data, numbering in the tens of thousands!

How in the world could physicians practice independently with such centralized, corporate power?

On November 6, 2007 we reached the end of the long corridor and entered the executive suite of United Healthcare's CEO. Soon, we were ushered into a conference room the likes of which I had never seen. The conference table must have been worth more than my house back in San Diego.

The 16 presidents, each in control of a multi-billion-dollar division of United Healthcare Group, all sat around the table, looking bored, yet dignified in their custom-tailored suits.

Mr. Burdick could not have been more gracious.

He truly wanted our effort to succeed. Jim Collins, my own CEO, began the technical presentation, designed to show how advanced services were being delivered in homes, with a surprise at the end. Jim was the perfect person both for me and for this presentation.

He was the former President/CFO of Scripps Clinic, the most prestigious medical group in San Diego with some $200 million in annual revenues.

Quickly, he went through our slides showing the concept of comprehensive medical care in the home as a response to urgent situations. With actual examples of our care, he compared the cost to the conventional hospital/ER alternative, an order-of-magnitude higher. At the end, he introduced me for our little surprise.

Unknown to the 16 presidents, now 15 since one had to excuse himself due to a viral crisis that was affecting his vineyards in Provence, I had wired myself with electrodes under my (cheap) suit, complete with a BlueTooth dongle sending my EKG, pulse rate and cardiac output flow metrics in real time to the projector screen.

With no visible wires or equipment, we all sat and watched my heart pump blood on the screen.

I told them what they all undoubtedly knew. Congestive heart failure was the number one cause of hospital admissions, readmissions, hospital days, and total cost of any disease in the United States.

It made intuitive sense to measure the flow rate of the failing heart in patients too weak to get to the office. They all knew such measurements were done routinely in the ICU, but none of them knew it could be done non-invasively anywhere, anytime, by anyone with a laptop and some amazing software.

Instead of changing medications based upon an often confusing physical exam; instead of relying on the patient's history from a group of patient's 70% of whom are demented; and instead of using the prevailing metric of "daily weights" to measure fluid retention in CHF patients generally too sick to stand on a scale, we had been measuring the cardiac output as a standard of care for only $42 per test, paid by Medicare in the home … for years.

Call Doctor had been included in a Medicare demonstration which compared our hospitalization results for heart failure patients to those of 749 office physician practices in the Western U.S. During the two-year study period, the overall annual re-admission rate for the 10,000 CHF patients in the study was 16%.

Only one of the 750 small group practices had a CHF readmission rate each year below 10%: Call Doctor.

Ours had been 0.8% over the two-year period.

Sam Ho, the President of Eldercare, quickly rose to the attack.

"I don't see why these patients can't be controlled with nurses on call and referral to outpatient clinic visits," he said.

"Because they cannot walk, cannot give a history, and often cannot know when their heart is failing until they are in extremis," I replied. "They need frequent and regular follow-up, even when they don't think they are getting sicker. Now, modern technologies exist wherein we can measure the true physiologic condition of patients just like we do in the intensive care unit."

I went on: "However, we don't need to stab their chest with a Swan-Ganz catheter threaded through their heart and have critical-care nurses inject fluids each time we want a measurement."

"With your help, we could actually monitor their critical life's function through a monitor sending signals like this not only to a Call Center, but to their physician in real-time. Only when necessary, the doctor, nurse or paramedic could be dispatched to the home for definitive treatment, as opposed to waiting for the panic of a 9-1-1 call."

Dr. Sam Ho abruptly got up and left after making an irrelevant, dismissive comment. I never found out whether his objections were real, or whether he also had French vineyards with an urgent viral infection.

And that was that.

Postscript: *Ken Burdick resigned in frustration a year after taking the most powerful executive position in civilian healthcare. He should be commended for trying, especially for publicly sharing his frustration at the failure to make such a huge, profitable company actually sensitive to the needs of sick patients.*

PART 6

The biggest challenges

CHAPTER 27

Precious little time

"The short flight offered no time for a patient history or scene description."

Growing up as a Navy brat had both advantages and disadvantages. The ten different schools I had attended before the ninth grade taught me the social skills of being a "military brat."

And I was.

My classmates never had time to get sick of me before Dad's promotions drove us to yet another East Coast submarine port. I had learned to make friends quickly and hold none too close so as to easily let go.

By the time I was in the ninth grade, Dad made Admiral and was to Naples, Italy. Eventually to command NATO's submarine fleet in the Mediterranean Sea. I was left in Virginia to attend a premier high school with an aging grandmother and her husband, who bled to death in front of me at home.

It was the perfect preparation for developing the self-confidence and personal skills eventually used in treating 30-to-40 patients each 12-hour shift in the emergency room. I never even saw their name, much less remembered them, but to this day I can tell you the potassium levels or blood gases of the most unstable ones.

Anyway, my grandmother had always said she thought there was just sawdust inside our stomachs. She had a rather simple philosophy about medicine, illustrated by the dark stain on the remnant of her index finger, the result of a kitchen amputation treated by sticking the severed stump in hot fireplace ash around 1910.

The ER is like that: Provide simple, quick stabilizing measures for vital, but relatively simple problems of lasting consequence.

For me, there was precious little time to become emotionally attached to either the patients or the practice of emergency medicine. For nearly a decade the night shifts at the trauma center or flying Life Flight missions had blurred into a hodgepodge of memories, few specific enough to deserve retelling.

One, however, does come to mind.

It was on a crystal-clear Saturday afternoon, sunny, blue sky, no humidity, no reason to worry about weather as the helicopter landed on the street downtown near the Navy's commercial loading dock.

"Man trapped in a machine" had been the call from dispatch.

When my beeper screamed, I was located in the ER. The short flight offered no time for a patient history or scene description, so I was surprised 12 minutes later, when the fireman directed me on-scene to a two-story ladder, saying, "He's up there, Doc. It's bad."

Climbing to the top of the huge ladder over the street, I leaned in a large window designed to allow industrial transfer of fertilizer ground fine by the six-inch rotating pipe on which had been welded large T-shaped tines a foot in length to mix the fertilizer which still dusted down from above.

In a small area the size of a two-door refrigerator lay a man groaning in Spanish, held erect by his right leg which had been wrapped twice around the six-inch pipe, his foot inserted into the remaining shards of his thigh-bone, melded into what was once a human leg.

His left leg poked out garishly to the other side, an open fracture of both shin bones still weeping slowly the little amount of blood he had left in his body.

Emergency medics from inside the building were above and behind the patient, working valiantly to rig a hoist under his armpits with which to lift him up off the pipe, but he was stuck.

One intravenous was running wide open in his left arm.

I had nothing I could do but start another IV through the large vein in his neck, collapsed as it was with little blood circulating to keep his peripheral veins open.

Then, the Life Flight nurse upon whom nearly all the lives depended, saved his life.

Phil Moomjean, RN, called from two stories down: "Doctor Bayne, do you want me to fly back to UCSD and get some blood?" I had not thought of this life-saving, totally-out-of-the-ordinary solution to our problem.

"Great idea," I called out, head muffled by the piles of fertilizer dust lying in the small room, soaking up what little blood my patient had left to offer. "We're gonna be here awhile."

At that time, I remember having an impure thought that embarrasses me today.

Even if he did survive, he was undoubtedly an "illegal" working off the grid who would have a life-long disfiguring injury and be a huge financial burden for the healthcare system.

Fortunately, years of training replaced the practical issues with what passed for instinct, so I joined in the fray and told the firemen I had found the problem.

When they lifted his body vertically, I could feel under his buttocks the prong that must've caught the cuff of his pants, spiraling first his foot, then his shin, then his knee and lower thigh as they wound around the powerful driveshaft.

The four-inch "tee" at the tip of the prong had inserted itself through the obturator foramen of his pelvis into his abdomen.

The poor man was hooked like a fish on a line.

I quickly amputated his leg above the knee with gloved hands and a pair of non-sterile bandage scissors, then put my right hand through the gaping hole in his buttocks to finger-dissect the pelvic bones free of the engaging metal.

Warning the firemen that as soon as the compression of the wrapped leg was relieved by extrication, he would lose all chance at a survivable blood pressure – after all, he had been pulseless since I had arrived. We would have to mule-haul him down the ladder to the street before even CPR could be started.

With no blood pressure, our bodies don't sense pain, so the garish procedures were done quickly without anesthesia. This must be what surgeons felt like in the Civil War, I thought to myself. Speed was key, not sterility or surgical technique.

As we clumsily lowered his lifeless body down the ladder and reached the street, the Life Flight helicopter was landing with six units of O-negative blood, the kind we can transfuse safely to almost anyone. Phil had already set up the infusion kits for two units and jumped out of the aircraft, stooped below the spinning blades which would have decapitated him.

With blood transfusions blasting in under pressure in both large-bore intravenous lines, I called my former Navy colleague who was now director of the UC San Diego Trauma Unit, and asked him to meet me in the Operating Room. The patient was unresponsive on full life-support but now had a slight chance of survival – thanks to the quick thinking of the flight nurse.

—◈—

Two years later, I got to meet the young man's lawyer at my deposition in support of his litigation against the company that made the defective safety switch on the fertilizer motor.

He was a naturalized U.S. citizen from Mexico who, when not in shock, spoke fluent English. He worked weekends to pay for his college classes, pursuing his degree from San Diego State University.

The surgeons had done their magic, albeit after a stormy course of gas gangrene and innumerable infectious complications from a perforated bowel, crushed by the invading tine in his belly.

He was now a college graduate, able to walk with crutches and a functional left leg, his right leg and buttocks replaced by an extensive prosthetic.

It felt good to describe the same gory details of his Life Flight rescue to six defense lawyers, who gradually turned pale with their own blood pooling somewhere distant to their brains. *That's* what was required to save this young man's life.

This is what we train for: a "save."

At that time, it was only the second field amputation in air-medical literature. Moreover, it represented what was most attractive to me about a medical career destined to travel to more uncontrolled and uncontrollable sites in patient's homes.

Instinctively, I knew that good training and experience will easily make the medical decisions rather straightforward in life-saving situations. But it's always the socio-environmental context of the situation which present the biggest challenges.

I couldn't get enough of it, not even after 500 flights.

CHAPTER 28

A shoebox full of mice

"My son just got into Harvard!"

In March of 1999, I was riding high.

The $5 million in the bank from a new round of financing provided stabilization and cashflow for Call Doctor, allowing us to hire 12 board-certified doctors who were making house calls daily just in San Diego.

There were nearly 100 employees managed by my brilliant Chief of Operations, Michelle Calleran.

Professionally speaking, she had been my "significant other" for years and had that unique ability to talk to doctors as an equal, so necessary in herding the cats of medicine.

On the floor, beneath my desk, I felt a gentle tug on my pants trousers, startling me.

The last time I had that feeling was as an intern driving my car across the San Diego-Coronado Bridge after buying a shoebox full of mice to feed my pet, a six-foot black rat snake. You see, the life of a surgical resident required having pets with which you wouldn't get emotionally involved.

That time, I had nearly driven off the bridge before the mouse that had decided to crawl up my pants leg thankfully changed directions and scampered downward. A few hours later, I ably persuaded it to exit my car.

This time, however, the tug was from Michelle's daughter, Sarah, a beautiful little rug rat whom we loved to have crawl around the office. She brought happiness and a dose of reality to the stress of the office environment.

As she flicked the cuff of my pants, the phone rang.

"I can't believe it!" I screamed moments later. "My son just got into Harvard!"

Perhaps a week later, I had already ordered the car sticker from Harvard and was making house calls in my ten-year-old Volvo station wagon. Nothing made me prouder than seeing "Harvard" on my rear windshield. I might have gotten into Harvard way back when – except for my grades.

Leaving the patient's home this time, I found myself being chased by a middle-aged venture capitalist. He was following me out to my car from his wife's bedside. It was my first house call to this home, and he wanted to know more about me.

I was in a hurry and was accustomed to patients or their family members asking how they could invest in Call Doctor, even on the first visit to a new patient.

His wife, suffering from a horrible neurologic disease that confined her to bed and crippled her deformed extremities into painful pretzels, was being cared for by this devoted husband.

All he had asked me to do was change the tracheostomy tube through which her ventilator connected her through her windpipe to life. Typically, such patients are in a hospital or nursing home, but she had been receiving expert care at home from her husband.

Each month, he dutifully had been taking her to the emergency room, where a doctor like myself changed the tracheostomy tube under controlled conditions. Like with most of anesthesia, it is a procedure that is usually routine, but can be punctuated by complications of utmost terror.

"Did you know I was an anesthesiologist before going into venture capital?" he asked.

"No, sir, I didn't," I replied. "No wonder your wife has been receiving such excellent care."

Noticing the crimson "Harvard" newly stickered to the rear window of my car, he suddenly exclaimed, "I bet that costs you a pretty penny."

"Yes," I replied, "My son just got accepted, so the financial challenge hasn't really started yet."

———⟊⟊⟊———

I suddenly remembered "Black Tuesday" back in 1996, when my daughter's tuition at Georgetown was higher than my entire adjusted gross income. Our two college kids would now be overlapping for one year, so my wife and I had started eating hot dogs and beans, again.

"How about I pay your son's tuition for the next four years?" he suddenly blurted. "All you have to do is come by every month and change my wife's endotracheal tube. As an anesthesiologist, I am also trained to do it, but if something went wrong, I couldn't live with myself."

I stopped getting into the car and backed myself out to the curb, standing next to him in the bright sunlight. Looking him straight in the eye, I said with a tone that must have mixed respect with a dose of anger welling up from somewhere hidden in my soul.

"Well, that would be delightful, but you would have to mail the checks to me in the federal penitentiary."

I went on to explain that it was now illegal for any doctor participating in Medicare – as 96% of all doctors did – to accept donations from patients.

It's a felony, a crime punishable by five years in jail and a $50,000 fine.

Then I added, "And to make sure you don't have access to better care because you're wealthy, they are enforcing that statute now."

At that moment, I was thinking of the young doctor in Seattle who had plea-bargained for a huge fine to avoid a jail sentence for making house calls. His "concierge" practice had billed patients for fees that were not allowed by Medicare, and he never "opted out" of his participation in Medicare payments.

Most of us cannot believe that physicians are subject to such austere restrictions in their right to provide services.

———

We parted amicably, and I promised to come back each month. If I wasn't available, someone else would come by, as we had trained everyone in trach tube replacement procedures, identical to those used in the emergency room.

As I drove away, I had a thought which has plagued me ever since: When a board-certified anesthesiologist with a second, successful career in venture capital cannot use his resources to secure the care he wants for his wife at home, how bad has U.S. healthcare policy become?

CHAPTER 29

Her name is Deirdre

"Females are certainly the tougher gender in almost every category."

I WAS SITTING OUTSIDE MY PATIENT'S HOUSE with the car's air conditioner going full blast. It was a Santa Ana day, one of those hot, dry windy days that supposedly makes people crazy.

Just when I parked the car, Bette Midler's "Wind Beneath My Wings" started playing, one of my favorite songs. Suddenly, I started sobbing, unable to get out of the car and see my patient.

It is funny how the important things in life lie waiting to ambush you when you least expect it. What had suddenly made me break down was the realization that this song, above all others, represented everything that is beautiful and truthful in my life.

Her name is Deirdre, and we were married as a rather typical Navy nurse/doctor pairing in 1975.

You can't imagine the life led by the spouse of an obsessive, ADHD-rattled serial entrepreneur like myself. I now recognize that the same genes which drive our extreme behaviors represent curses for our spouse, or, as the case may be, ex-spouses.

Yet, if an entrepreneur is fortunate enough to be married to a woman like Deirdre, he might have a chance at marital success, painful as the process is at times.

When anyone asks how long I've been married, I like to put it this way: Deirdre and I have been happily married for 44 years now. We

We actually got married nearly 50 years ago, but there were a few years when we weren't speaking to each other."

⸺◦◦◦⸺

Seriously, females are in the process of taking over the medical profession in America. Thank God for that.

Because we males have screwed it up so thoroughly there has to be some sort of major change in the offing, and a gender-based change of command is as good as any.

As of 2018, the majority of medical students are female. Increasingly, females are in the majority for most specialty-training programs, even the surgical programs that have fed the male ego over the eons.

Perhaps this new wave of female physicians will find solutions to the problems a male-dominated healthcare system has left as our legacy.

An age-matched female over 75 years old with two chronic diseases has a 20% chance of having a relative at home providing caregiving duties. A male in the same situation has an 80% chance of being cared for by a loved one.

The reasons for this disparity are many, all related to gender.

First, the gap in lifespan for American men and women has expanded to at least six years, so the men are mostly dead by the age of 75 – or too infirm themselves to provide constructive help for a disabled wife.

What's more, disabilities strike men sooner in life than women, although a better way to describe the phenomenon is that women are simply tougher.

As an example, the average age of women getting hip replacements is several years older than men. Studies show that the only relevant variable is that women have a higher threshold to pain.

Females are certainly the tougher gender in almost every category. Perhaps that is why God has us create 105 live male births for every 100 live female births in the United States. Death rates of male fetuses are much higher than female fetuses, as well, so the ratio of male conceptions is actually much higher than female zygotes.

Centenarians are doubling every 13 years now, and 90% of them are female. Anyone who has bought life insurance, disability insurance, or invested in a lifetime annuity knows about the disparity in male longevity. I have spent entire days making house calls without seeing a patient with an age of only two-digits –and they are ALL female, all the time.

There are many reasons for the durability of the gender which bears and cares for our children, but evolutionary selection seems to cover the root cause. For example, we know that male mitochondrial DNA mutations are more likely to kill you than ones which occur in the female.

Hence, unlike the unstable and dangerously flawed male mitochondrial DNA, only the much more stable mitochondrial DNA from the mother is passed on to the child.

Of the 72 common causes of death, all but six are more likely to occur in men at younger ages than women. Men die by violence, suicide, and accidents at rates over twice that of women. Cardiac disease, the number one cause of death in men and women in America, causes death much earlier in a man's life than a woman's life.

Several years ago, I researched our emergency medicine literature and found some astounding statistics. As compared to an age-matched male in the U.S., a woman having their first heart attack is:

Half as likely to be taking prophylactic aspirin;

Half as likely to reach the ER within the 4-hour window needed for successful use of the magic "clot-buster" drugs;

Half as likely to be correctly diagnosed as having a heart attack;

Half as likely to get a percutaneous angioplasty (the procedure used to stop the progression of damage in a heart attack and prevent new ones);

Twice as likely to require an open-chest coronary artery bypass operation;

And, as a result, twice as likely to die.

Certainly, Alexis de Tocqueville was right back in 1810 when he reported back to Europe on how those lowly frontier colonials had created a society robust enough to conquer the most powerful army and navy in the world during the Revolution.

Here's what he wrote: "America is built on the strong backs of its women."

CHAPTER 30

It was a genuine smile

"There was no question she was present in all our conversations."

THE GUILT I FELT AS I TURNED LEFT in my familiar neighborhood was stronger than usual. Mrs. Garraway wasn't sick, but I just knew I needed to check on her. This special lady lived in the back bedroom of a modest one-floor house near my home.

The door was always unlocked, and her son worked, so she stayed alone, accompanied only by her wide-screen TV and number of parrot-like birds kept in cages that she could see though the back window.

Mrs. Garraway had multiple sclerosis, an incurable disease that had already taken its toll. Not that she appeared to notice or care.

Whenever I came into her bedroom, I'd almost forget why I came. The reason was her smile, luminous and welcoming.

You would think a disease that gradually paralyzed every muscle in your body over the years would make one bitter, or at least depressed.

But not Mrs. Garraway. She was always smiling, and it wasn't the smile of "risor sardonicus," a contortion caused by other forms of progressive paralysis. It was a genuine smile, one of good cheer, and it always made my day.

That day, I needed cheering up. Funding had run out, again, on our business of propagating house calls. This time, it wasn't a question of "strategic undercapitalization," so that the vulture capitalists could gain voting control over our board of directors by buying new stock.

It was 1995 and the first three rounds of venture capital had run their course.

A subsidy to the physician's salaries would be necessary to keep the six doctors making visits with me on board. I had to find another source of cash, and quick. You can't expect a physician burdened by an average of $250,000 in medical school debt to work for next for nothing.

Most doctors loved being free of the tyranny of office appointments stacked up months in advance, but they also had mortgages and children who were going to college. Without some form of cash infusion, my house of cards was about to crumble.

I needed a boost, and Mrs. Garraway was as certain a source for it as there was in my life.

"Well, hello," she greeted me, lying prostrate in her brightly-colored muumuu, staring straight ahead. Her neck was frozen with a gaze down and to the right, where the television was.

Her son had invented a little pressure switch she could operate with the one remaining digit that still worked – the little pinky on her right hand. A baseball game was on TV.

"Did you come to help my Padres beat up on those awful Pittsburgh Pirates?"

Mrs. Garraway could quote every player's batting average on the San Diego Padres, along with other statistics I never had time to learn growing up.

"No, ma'am, I was in the area and just thought I would drop by," I began. "I haven't seen you in a couple of months and just wanted to make sure your medical needs were met. It is getting to be Fall, and I brought a flu shot for you."

I sat down, the parrots behind the open window started their loud squawking. It stopped as soon as Mrs. Garraway issued a loud, but peaceful swishing sound.

"How thoughtful," she said over the ever-present smile.

With her neck frozen, she never seemed to take her eyes off the baseball game, but there was no question she was present in all our conversations. In taking an interim history and checking her posterior for bedsores, I noticed a paleness to her gums and soft tissues.

I wanted to ask her if she had been feeling weaker than usual, or felt dizzy when sitting up, but it made no sense. She spent 24 hours a day paralyzed in bed, propped up about 30 degrees at her head.

"You look like you might have lost a little weight since I last saw you," I offered.

"Maybe," she replied. "I don't have much appetite, but Billy says it will make it easier to turn me when he changes the sheets and such."

I drew a blood sample to send to the lab for a CBC (complete blood count) as a reflex, then gave her the flu shot. There really wasn't much concern, but when patients are so defenseless the usual presenting complaints of many diseases are masked.

One of the tests I no longer found "dispositive" in the home setting was the white cell count, part of a CBC. It rarely makes a difference in any acute medical decision if you are thorough in your exam and have time to listen to a patient's full history.

We chatted for a few moments.

She always asked about my plans for a national expansion of the Call Doctor model for house call services. As one of only a very few patients with whom I shared such information, she was able to pry out of me the news that had me so concerned.

"We are out of money, and tomorrow the money guys are flying in with a presentation for continued financing that will probably be onerous," I told her.

On a roll, I went on: "As you know from looking at your Medicare Explanation of Benefits bills, they still pay very little for our services and often refuse any payment for the lab and things like flu shots. Our efforts to change the regulations in Washington are tracking, but nothing seems likely to start fair payment by Medicare any time soon."

"Well, honey," she continued. "You just tell President Clinton that

I said he should listen to you more carefully. I would have been hospitalized a dozen times in the past without your visits."

And there it was.

The Garraway Effect soon had me smiling broadly as I left her house, blood vial in hand.

I went home feeling much better, spun the blood sample in a centrifuge kept for that purpose, and placed it in a packet with the lab requisition for the nightly pick-up. Performing such a simple favor for such a special patient was a guaranteed happy pill.

Surely, the meeting tomorrow would work itself out.

Mrs. Garraway died precipitously at home a few weeks later. The blood sample had come back with a white count over 50,000, a low platelet count, and marked anemia. She had acute leukemia. I only saw her once more, when she took the option for no further care.

The reality of her advanced MS made her decision completely understandable, but I remember pushing harder than I should have for a referral to oncology for treatment.

During my last conversation with Mrs. Garraway, the smile never left her face.

"Don't you worry about me, Honey," she called after me as I walked from her bedroom for what would be the last time. "I've had a good life!"

Her spirit made my funding problems seem inconsequential. Just seeing patients with such courage was payment enough.

CHAPTER 31

Not being sufficiently conscious

*"I knew all about helium and its ability
to make you sound like Donald Duck."*

CAREER TRANSITIONS WERE HARD for my generation. We were raised in the '50s, when families rarely moved, prices never changed, and you bought one car that you drove until it died, hopefully after you did.

Same for our careers. You trained for a single occupation, got hired, and stayed employed there for the rest of your life. Or so you planned.

However, job transitions were socially acceptable, unlike changes in religion and college, or wives. The book *Psychocybernetics* was popular, espousing author Dr. Maxwell Maltz's theory that it was in the struggle to succeed that we found happiness, not in the success itself.

I loved the book, because it explained why every time I had reached a modicum of success I became nervous, irritable, perhaps unhappy. I had spent my life seeking approval from those around me, but when I got to a level of success where I had earned it, I soon found myself moving on.

Some of us need attention more than others.

I suspect this applies to career success as well as social acceptance. In my case, the need was insatiable, which has led to some unusual events that nearly killed me. Sometimes, the need to feel special had a significant price to pay.

It was this insecurity that followed me into the ballroom as I escorted my wife to the black-tie party at the University Club, a week before Christmas in 1982.

I had just finished my Navy career as Chairman of the world's largest military emergency department, so felt rather special being recruited for the academic faculty at the University of California at San Diego.

Dr. George Shumake, one of my staff ER physicians in the Navy, had left to go to UCSD the year before and said the career potential there was great. He was the only person I knew in the entire department of some 50 doctors and nurses.

The ER Director had invited me to the gala to meet the staff at their annual dinner-dance. He said he planned to introduce me to the Vice Chancellor of the University of California, a real privilege for me. They were all sitting across the ballroom floor on a raised dais as my wife and I entered the large room fashionably late.

Feeling nervous, I noticed Dr. Shumake standing in the corner on my side of the room. He was talking to an employee who was filling colored balloons from an orange helium tank used for decorations.

"Let's go see George," I said to my wife. "He'll know what the protocol is for meeting the Vice Chancellor."

Standing by the orange tank, George briefed me on the dignitaries across the room. "All the academic bigwigs are here," he said, making me even more self-conscious.

It was then, for reasons known only to psychiatrists and behavioral therapists, that a brilliant idea suddenly jumped into my addled mind.

"Why don't I go over to meet them talking like Donald Duck?" I asked George.

Dr. Shumake was one of those doctors you want to see when they are cutting off your skivvies in the trauma room. He had the best judgment of any physician I ever worked with. Perhaps I should have noticed the quixotic look on his face as I began taking the full balloons and inhaling the helium from them.

My thinking, clouded by nervous anxiety, was that since UCSD had hired me to start their new Hyperbaric Treatment Center, perhaps I should demonstrate my competence from three years spent as the senior medical officer at the Navy's School of Diving and Salvage.

We often used helium wash-out curves to flush out a diagnosis of occult small-airway disease in prospective Navy divers. Point is, I knew all about helium and its ability to make you sound like Donald Duck.

What I didn't know was that the orange tanks we filled with 80% helium and 20% oxygen in the Navy looked exactly like the pure helium tanks used in the party balloon industry. After all, you don't need oxygen in a party balloon.

Let me explain.

When your blood oxygen level gets really low (hypoxia) while you keep your carbon dioxide level normal, you tend to feel pretty good, even giddy. So giddy, in fact, you can make some dumb decisions. It is why pilots must wear an oxygen mask when flying above 10,000 feet.

As Dr. Shumake and my embarrassed wife looked on, I inhaled deeply from balloon after balloon, only exhaling between balloons. Eventually, I was feeling pretty terrific, unaware that the cause of my sudden confidence was a dangerously low blood-oxygen level.

"Let's go," I told my wife in my best Donald Duck voice.

I figured I should hold my breath as I walked across the ballroom floor, being careful to conserve the lung-full of pure helium I now held, but unaware I had not been breathing any oxygen for a few minutes.

The last thing I remember was the ER chairman leaning over to the Vice-Chancellor to whisper something in his ear.

In my hypoxic mind he was probably saying, "Here comes our new Associate Director of Emergency Medicine. He's the perfect person to head up our new Hyperbaric Treatment Center ..."

Just as I reached the front of the raised dais, my grand-mal convulsion started, a typical result when your brain suddenly finds itself without enough oxygen to work properly. Seizures due to low oxygen levels will continue until the brain re-oxygenates and are often associated with incontinence, creating a mess to clean up.

Now I must admit I wasn't conscious for most of the real excitement, but I have many times since imagined how surreal it must have been to watch 50 emergency physicians and specialty nurses gather around me.

My wife of more than four decades still won't talk to me about this, but I know at least some of them competed for the right to run my resuscitation. I do remember vaguely waking up to hear someone saying: "Did anyone ever actually call 9-1-1?"

Fortunately, you can't hold your breath when you are seizing. (God thought of everything.) The short seizure allowed enough oxygen in the room air to reach my lungs, thus entering my bloodstream. I woke up lying in my tuxedo on the ballroom floor, still a bit groggy.

What I remember clearly is that I didn't have any pulse, so the various professors were quite flummoxed as to what to do. My low oxygen levels had also caused some sort of life-threatening arrhythmia. Every time I tried to sit up, I started to faint again, so I laid back down.

Before long, I had breathed enough oxygen to hear the shouts directed to my attention. They varied from "Are you all right?" to "Are you having chest pain?"

Still quite hypoxic, I thought this was funny, as I realized what had happened, but I still couldn't talk for another few minutes.

Finally, my heart rhythm converted into something more compatible with life, so I answered the crowd with my very best rendition of a Donald Duck voice: "I feel like shit."

My barely intelligible, garbled voice fostered another round of intense medical conjecture.

Exotic theories were murmured like, "Did he rupture his larynx and have an air embolism?" You probably know that academic physicians live for their reputation as brilliant diagnosticians, so everyone probably wanted to be the first to the goal.

As for me, I was still feeling high from the hypoxia, as well as smug, knowing exactly what had happened but not being sufficiently conscious to become embarrassed.

The sad truth is, I enjoyed being the center of attention.

—◦◦◦—

Much has been written about this sort of transition from life to near-death and back, even without the tunnel-of-light experience so often described. Having the benefit of hindsight, I believe it is a lot like the arc of our lives.

We struggle to achieve, then have trouble accepting a modicum of success, and often screw things up so we can start all over again.

Dr. Maltz was right: It *is* in the struggle that we find fulfillment. The harder part is living with success.

However, each time the cybernetic cycle renews, we are armed with new insight, new information to use in controlling our fears, our anxieties about life … and death. So, the pattern continues as a tapestry of constantly changing fractals, building on what has gone before.

Mine has been a history of striving, especially since it didn't kill me.

Pleasure boating gave me the background to build custom vans to support lab and X-ray in patient's driveways. The Navy gave me the discipline and experience to run a company. Surgery training gave me confidence. Emergency medicine gave me the wide horizon you need in handling things you've never encountered before.

My church gave me repose during the many trials and tribulations of nine venture capital rounds. Reading the Bible in retirement (finally) gave me the perspective that it was never really about me.

—◦◦◦—

As I sat on the ballroom floor in front of the dais, Dr. Shumake finally put things together and must have explained the event to everyone as I slowly rose to a chair, if not the occasion.

The crowd around the new Associate Director of Emergency Medicine soon dissipated, and my hypoxic high morphed into a well-deserved embarrassment. My pulses returned with vigor. The ambulance was cancelled and Dr. Shumake won the funny bone prize.

Ever the jokester, George leaned over to me and whispered in my ear, "I have some good news."

"Whah?" I said with just a hint of Donald Duck.

"At least you weren't incontinent," he said with a slight smirk.

PART 7

Being there

CHAPTER 32

The doorbell effect

*"It is no wonder patients love the concept
of having a physician come to their home."*

THE THRESHOLD OF THE HOME IS A HOLY ONE. Memorialized in the
Hippocratic Oath, a physician crosses the threshold to enter the patient's home "to see the man...just the man."

The Romans thought this border was so important they created a
god for it, named Janus. Today, "Janus-faced" means two-faced, but
to the Romans, Janus was a two-headed god.

One Janus head faced into the home to protect its inhabitants. The
other Janus head faced outward, guarding those that leave the house
or, perhaps those who remain in the house from outsiders.

Physicians would do well to consider the concept of this ancient
Janus-faced god before committing themselves to a life in mobile
medicine.

I tend to think of this important threshold as the "Doorbell Effect."

When we ring the patient's doorbell, we have already made a huge
concession to the patient by coming to their home or workplace. Especially if the patient's problem is acute, we have dropped everything
just on the contingency that they need our professional services,
knowing that most of the time it isn't an emergency.

By responding to the patient's home either urgently or on a scheduled house call, the doctor is showing respect for the patient's needs

beyond the pale. In every other physician encounter, the patient has made all of the sacrifices for transport.

They have made the decision to seek care, arranged transportation, given up any hope of financial controls in the case of the emergency room, and often waited patiently (too long?) for the office visit.

Normally, patients have scheduled the office visit, found the doctor's address, paid for travel in various ways, accounted for navigation in some manner, suffered from their lack of control over weather and delays in the doctor's office, not to mention paying for expenses like gas, oil, tolls, insurance, and accommodations for infirmities requiring wheelchairs, splints, painful transfers, leaking wound dressings, and so on.

The sicker a patient is, the harder these routine issues are to handle successfully.

It is no wonder patients love the concept of having a physician come to their home. In the category of patients most appropriate for house calls (the multi-morbid, non-ambulatory chronically ill), it is not so important for the doctor to keep a strict time schedule for appointments. Our patients are going to be "home" whether we are on time or not.

One of our advertising consultants suggested the ditty: "The doctor's waiting room is your living room."

In sum, the simple fact a doctor rings your doorbell has changed the healthcare equation in profoundly important ways … all in favor of the patient.

In return, what the doctor receives is a predictable and instant granting of the patient's trust. Although they seem unaware of the lack of any reimbursement for the time and cost of a doctor's travel, patients know that coming to their home is a special privilege given to them by the physician, and they repay us with trust.

They trust us to come on the morning or the afternoon we promise … or call if we are delayed. They trust us to protect them from harm by not leaving them in the lurch with a significant, acute problem wherein delay incurs risk.

Most importantly, they trust us to come back when we say we will. And that may be the most cost-effective and largely-untapped tool in healthcare reform.

——⟿——

The contingency cost of "being there when they need you" is hard to quantify.

When I built my first Mobile Physician Treatment Center (MPTC) in 1984, I had no operating capital, so the van was parked in my driveway.

Over the next two-year period I met neighbors I didn't know I had, received accolades I didn't quite deserve, and grew anxious when strangers told me, "I always knew I could call you when I had an emergency."

CHAPTER 33

Home alone

"I sat amidst the flowers and presented the options."

THE FIRST HOUSE CALL I EVER MADE with the full support of the MPTC with its lab and X-ray capability came the week after I met some potential investors at a formal dinner party.

Clare Tavares, after whom the San Diego neighborhood of Clairemont was named (or so she claimed; history says otherwise), had fallen from a ladder in her La Jolla garden. She called from where she lay, outside in the flowers and dirt of her beautiful garden.

A quick history suggested a non-life-threatening "fall with injury," so I arrived about 30 minutes later.

Clare lay on her back, uncomfortable with pelvic pain if she moved anything below the waist, but her pain was controlled if she didn't move. My exam quickly suggested a pelvic fracture, so I rolled in the portable X-ray unit, placed an X-ray cassette under her pelvis, and shot the first X-ray even done on a house call.

It was 1985.

Developed in the van using wet-film processing, the X-ray confirmed a non-placed fracture of her pelvis in two places.

Since this type of fracture is associated with bleeding sometimes, I did some blood tests to rule out hemorrhage, as well as any electrolyte problems or dehydration, which might have caused her to fall.

With her entire ER work-up done in less than an hour, I sat

amidst the flowers and presented the options. Normally, an ambulance is called to admit her to the hospital for pain control and nursing support.

However, since all the ER tests had been done on scene, we could directly admit her to her orthopedist on the ward.

This option had the advantages of letting her select her own specialist (or ask me for a referral), avoiding the "lights and sirens" of a 9-1-1 ambulance, and guaranteed that she went to a hospital of her choice, versus "the nearest appropriate facility."

But Clare was a smart woman.

"What if I stayed home?" she asked.

"Pelvic fractures hurt a lot," I replied, "but I can give you medicine to control the pain for the first few weeks. If your bowels lock up, as they sometimes do with this injury, we should limit you to a liquid diet the first 24 hours, and I can arrange for home health nurses to be with you the first day, and check on you as often as you need thereafter.

Then I added: "Of course, if anything goes bump in the night, you can always call 9-1-1 or ask me to come back if it is not life-threatening."

Like almost every one of the 10,000 patients I have seen in such situations, Clare opted for home health, staying home and maintaining control over her life and own environment.

—⁓—

The elderly woman, let's call her Gladys, reached under her pillow to show me her opiate pain killers. I had developed the habit of counting pills in the bottle and matching the "pill count" to the known prescriptive history.

This time, however, I asked Gladys why she kept her pills under her pillow.

"So my grandson won't steal them and sell them to his friends," was all she said.

Her grandson turned out to be running a major drug ring out of the lady's back bedroom. She didn't know this, as the hospital bed to which she was confined for life – was located in the only room in the house big enough to cope with it: Her living room.

Without telling her, I called the police later that day.

———

On another occasion, I was gloved up and debriding (cutting away dead tissue) a bedsore of an elderly female when the doorbell rang.

The patient was bedbound from multiple diseases with names like polymyositis, a condition in which the body senses that the muscles are foreign invaders and proceeds to destroy itself.

The door was answered by her ten-year-old great-granddaughter, who luckily for me was bilingual.

She represented one of the five generations of females living ion this modest single-family home.

To my surprise, I heard a deep-throated male voice.

"I need to ask you to stay at home and not leave this house until I come back and give you permission."

Pus dripped from my gloves as I hurried to the front door, only to find a huge SWAT team member, armored vest and black helmet in place, bristling with weapons and standing in the way.

He told me they were performing a raid on the crack house next door, and that things "might get ugly, so I need you to stay inside."

I don't normally think about the stressors in a patient's life with this level of graphic realism, even when I am in the emergency room treating the entrails of such activities. Later, this patient allowed her picture to be taken for a two-page article in *Forbes* magazine, but we told the media only part of the story.

In cases such as these, your heart simply goes out to your patient. It goes out involuntarily and completely, because you know you are going home to your middle-class, mostly white neighborhood that's devoid of such issues. It goes out because you don't ever worry about getting shot and you know dinner is waiting for you when you get home.

Perhaps it goes out because you know that by being mobile you can actually do something to make this patient's life a little better.

What you can do is assure the patient that you are coming back. That you understand now how hard it must be for her and her grandchildren and great-grandchildren to handle her diseases, her bedsores, her pain, her likely demise lurking behind all of them. You tell her you understand, and you will come back to check her bedsores and other matters in a week.

Even now, that is really all that most of my patients want: *They want to know that I will come back.*

The relief you see in their moist eyes is, at first, missed. What you see mostly is the ego-gratifying gratefulness they, and their loved ones, shower on you as you try to leave to go to the next patient's home. I warn the doctors I train in house call medicine that the gratification is obscuring the reality of the patient's plight.

More importantly, it can be clouding their understanding of what you can, and can't do, and it is in the what you can't do that problems lurk hidden, waiting to harm, even kill the patient who was so grateful to you.

I lecture more inexperienced mobile clinicians to beware of what I call "The Great White Knight Syndrome." The patient wants their doctor up on a cloud so they can trust us.

Normally, that trust is limited to the exercises available in the office environment: things such as writing prescriptions, ordering lab tests, scheduling the next appointment.

When you make urgent house calls, however, such trust can easily be assumed for having the right medicine with you at the time, doing the lab test at the same visit on a portable instrument, thus making follow-up "just for lab results" unnecessary by generating immediate X-ray results.

These things can be expected, and should be delivered with each and every house call in an urgent situation.

CHAPTER 34

Like the Michelin Man

"I arrived slowly, face down with blood
pouring out of my ears and nose."

DURING MY BRIEF TENURE as Senior Medical Officer of the Navy School of Diving and Salvage in Panama, Florida, I was asked by the Deputy Chief of Naval Operations to go to England and learn how the British escape from submarines stranded on the bottom.

The U.S. had already spent over $2 billion on the Deep Submergence Rescue Vehicle, and it didn't work. The ever-pragmatic British had a different approach.

Since all but two of the 104 submarines which had sunk in peacetime had sunk over the continental shelf (average depth less than 1,000 feet), they had been experimenting with a "blow and go" free ascent.

They had a successful technique up to 750 feet, although at that depth a couple of their experimental subjects came to the surface blind from decompression sickness, or oxygen toxicity. Nobody knew which.

I was trained and selected for my 300-foot free ascent from the *HMS Survivor*, a British nuclear submarine that sat on the bottom of the ocean off Scotland. Knowing it was cold topside, and that I was the first to go, I outsmarted and almost killed myself.

I took my down jacket and pushed it into the small space allowed by the tight-fitting submarine immersion suit down between my legs. Still in the research phase, the Brits asked me to strap on a barograph recorder to my upper arm, keeping track of time and depth of the ascent. The recorder allowed us to reconstruct what happened later.

The normal ascent rate using the British system was about 10 feet per second, so I was expected on the surface in 30 seconds. After two minutes passed, the British were in a panic.

Where was the American naval doctor? At 2:22 min, I arrived slowly, face down with blood pouring out of my ears and nose.

Without any delay, the SEAL-like support team in the inflatable quickly grabbed me, threw me to the bottom of the boat and raced to the surface-support vessel. Less than 60 seconds later, I found myself in the ship's decompression chamber – at 165 feet on compressed air, beginning a Treatment Table 6A (the "A" stands for Air Embolism).

The nitrogen narcosis of a deep air-dive quickly cleared, and I realized I was making a repetitive air dive to 165 feet immediately after a 300-foot bounce dive. Suffice to say, I knew this was a dive profile for which we have never had anything close to a safe decompression schedule.

The proposed treatment itself was a life-threatening exposure. I felt fine.

What had happened was the result of my ignorance of Archimedes' principle: Water is displaced by any object whose relative weight determines the attitude of the object.

In other words, my down jacket, which made me look like the Michelin Man, displaced a much heavier amount of water, so my butt lifted immediately upon release from the submarine at 300 feet.

The British dry suit had a clear plastic hood over the face, which released the expanding air into a small life vest from the bottom.

As I sashayed my way up slowly from the butt-first attitude my down jacket provided, the face shield ruptured at 220 feet, reducing my buoyancy significantly and prolonging my ascent by almost two minutes.

The blood from my nose and ears was insignificant, as ruptured ear drums were a common problem due to the rapid, compression rate used. However, the British manual mistakenly used such blood as an indication of air embolism.

Hence, the dramatic rescue and emergency recompression on a seven-hour Treatment Table 6A for Air Embolism.

The real problem was my new decompression obligation from being on a repeat dive to extraordinary depth, even in a dry chamber.

As with our own Navy procedures, the British Master Diver in charge of the recompression was not allowed to take orders from anyone inside the chamber, no matter their credentials.

Since there was no other diving medical expert present, it took a call to the Pentagon to convince him that I had not embolized.

That also convinced him that I would undoubtedly be paralyzed or killed unless he brought the chamber up to 60 feet, where I could breathe oxygen safely and avoid the bends.

Fortunately, he did.

PART 8

In the beginning

CHAPTER 35

Man of the house

"Dad, how long have you been in the Navy?"

BECAUSE OF DAD'S FAR-FLUNG OVERSEAS DUTIES, HE WASN'T HOME
the way I am. Let me finish with a few stories of my childhood and
early adult life.

For one thing, each of my parents died too young and because of
Dad's far-flung overseas duties, he wasn't home all that much. In fact,
from the time I had finished the 9th grade back home in Virginia, I
rarely ever saw him.

Living with my overwhelmed mother and her own parents in
Norfolk, Virginia, I responded typically.

Which is to say, I mostly rebelled.

To my adolescent way of thinking, while Mom and Dad were enjoying what I imagined was nothing less than the Italian Riviera at
the U.S. Navy base in Naples, it was unfair that I was watching my
mother's legless father bleed to death from diabetic complications.

Soon enough, my mother opted to join my father in Italy and
elsewhere, leaving me alone with my grandmother during my high
school years, which I spent attending a top prep school.

I'm sure none of this seemed like a hardship to my Dad, since his
own father had conceived him while on leave from a tuberculosis
sanitorium in Kentucky during World War I. Much later, I learned
that Dad had never even lived with his father under the same roof.

He spoke of his parents only rarely. He said his Mother died of "Quinsey sore throat," which is what they called strep in the 1930s. He never spoke of his father other than to say he was sickly and died when Dad was 8 years old.

Dad's story was that he was raised by his Aunt Zola and his grandmother, a person I remember only as this ancient, bed-bound hypochondriac.

—◦◦◦—

Yet, somehow my father became a great man.

Today, we calculate the negative impact of such early traumatic experiences as an ACE score, shorthand for Adverse Childhood Experiences. Measuring difficult types of physical and mental abuse, neglect and other factors, the range goes from 1 to 10.

The higher the score, the greater likelihood of serious health issues later in that child's life.

For example, a score of 4 or more is associated with a 17-fold increase in drug abuse, along with a doubling of the likelihood you will spend time in jail, a doubling of the chance for heart attacks and strokes, and a five-fold increase in certain other diseases.

My father's ACE score would've been 6.

You could never have predicted my father would become the youngest Navy Admiral ever selected who had not attended the Naval Academy. You would not have predicted my father would have two Distinguished Service Medals and three Legion of Merit Medals, the second- and third-highest medals awarded in peacetime.

You would not have thought he would be appointed by President Nixon to negotiate the international treaty with Bahrain that made him the first Commander of the U.S. Middle East forces.

For reference, that was the job General Norman Schwarzkopf made famous and led the Central Command for the Iraqi wars.

Nor would you have predicted President Ford would stand beside my father to sign a Presidential Order making Dad the first President of the National Defense University. As for me, sitting next to the

Chairman of the Joint Chiefs and meeting President Ford that day left me dumbstruck.

While I was still in grade school, my father was hosting the King and Queen of Iceland, along with the future King of Spain for dinner on one of his submarines.

While I was in high school, Dad spent a week sleeping on a cot in the White House War Room next to Bobby Kennedy during the Cuban Missile Crisis, helping the Secretary of the Navy save the world from nuclear Armageddon.

While I was in college, Dad was appointed the first NATO Commander of Submarines, Mediterranean, living in Naples, Italy. His career was one of meteoric success and significant firsts.

Every command he had, he left it changed for the better, usually in no small way.

Perhaps, I often ask myself, my need to seek change is genetic?

—◦◦◦—

Three years ago, in 2018, an elderly woman called me out of the blue and said she had found a box of letters in her aunt's house back in Norfolk, Virginia, where Dad was raised.

She said she had recognized Dad's name – it's hard to forget the mouthful "Vice-Admiral Marmaduke Gresham Bayne" – and found me on the Internet.

She went on to tell me the large box contained daily love letters between my Dad's parents over the nine years it took my grandfather to die from what was then called "consumption."

Even with the passing of nearly 100 years, reading those letters was painful. Dad had never mentioned them and I'm not even sure he knew about them, although each made direct reference to Dad and his brother, two years younger.

Here's a sample: "Now, Gresham, Daddy is still sick, so you have to be the Man of the House for a while. Make sure Mommy is getting her rest and don't forget your chores … each and every day. Daddy needs to know you are taking care of Mommy and your brother while he gets well."

When he got that letter, Dad was six years old.

Apparently, Aunt Zola had kept these letters after my grandfather died. A few years later, Dad's mother couldn't take it anymore on the $100 monthly pension given WWI veterans and abandoned her family. Dad never used the word "orphan" in his life.

Not once.

———

Eventually, I finished my own education by going to medical school on a Navy scholarship and getting assigned to a straight surgical internship at Balboa Hospital in San Diego.

Driving into the city that first memorable day I was struck by the natural beauty of what we presumptuously call "America's Finest City."

Before I even registered at the Navy's Bachelor Officers Quarters, I stopped at a pay phone (it was July 1, 1973), and called Dad at the National War College.

It took a bit of work to get past his secretary and the other aides screening my call because he was busy briefing Sen. Eugene McCarthy, a Presidential candidate that year. Eventually, Dad answered, his voice full of concern: "Yes, son, is everything all right?"

"Dad," I said, "How long have you been in the Navy?" There was a pregnant pause as my father thought about how to take this question.

"Thirty-two years. Why do you ask?"

"Well, I've been in the Navy one day, and I'm already living better than you!"

Then, I hung up the phone abruptly.

We laughed about that years later, but it reflected my lack of understanding of Exodus 20:12 ("Honor thy father and mother") and the Navy's Core Values of "Honor, courage, commitment."

Dad represented both, and so much more. But it wasn't until he retired that I learned what a great man he was.

And what those words really mean.

CHAPTER 36

Thick chocolate shake

"He was only conflicted about how God would receive him."

I REMEMBER CLEARLY THAT AUGUST DAY in 1971 when I first sensed that my father was dying.

We were in a French helicopter flying into the volcano that formed Isle de la Reunion, a small island nation in the middle of the Indian Ocean. Dad was being given a VIP tour of the island courtesy of the Governor-General and I was a tagalong as a first-year medical student from Virginia.

Dad suddenly spoke into his headset: "OK, we've had enough. Let's go back, now, as fast as you can."

We landed at the small, provincial airport, and Dad literally ran from the aircraft into the terminal. Years later, I found out that was when his bladder cancers bled for the first time.

It began the important part of my relationship with my father that lasted for 37 years. It was the year I began to realize that my father was truly an honorable man.

After President Jimmy Carter forced his medical retirement, Dad spent three decades fighting primary cancers that never stopped coming.

Between trips to the Portsmouth Naval Hospital for more surgery, his time was spent building outhouses for poor blacks in rural Virginia, raising money for a white social services department that still ignored the poor, mostly-black farmers.

He would call to tell me great stories of how they had built a new church or traded religious services with the local black church. Only rarely would he ask me for medical advice on how to treat the pastor, who was once found walking naked and babbling incoherently on a North Carolina beach.

He would only call about his own medical problems in extremis, like the time he had to pull off the road he was shaking so badly. I told him to call 9-1-1, as he described the onset of sepsis, a life-threatening infection that often kills the elderly.

In watching my father constantly facing death during the 25 years of his medical struggles, I learned that *courage* really was putting your fate in the hands of a Higher Power.

I learned that a *commitment* to teaching Sunday School can be as important as teaching the admirals and generals who will lead our Armed Forces into future conflicts.

I learned that his friends cried real tears at his funeral and called him "a most *honorable* man."

The day Dad stopped his dialysis and resigned himself to certain death, he was only conflicted about how God would receive him. "I can't believe my God would want me to live a life that is nothing more than suffering."

His only complaint was: "I can't do anything for anyone anymore."

Having known this moment was coming, I counselled him as I would any patient.

"Dad, you really don't have to go to dialysis. People stop it all the time when they decide it is a life not worth living."

His countenance suddenly brightened up. Soon, Leroy came into his room in the nursing hospital to take him to dialysis. Leroy, Dad said, was a "fine young man with a bright future."

Dad told me Leroy had gotten all the way through ninth grade and was proud of his responsibilities in taking patients to and from the near-by dialysis center. Driving patients around was a job that represented his highest hopes, Dad had said, "But he can do more, I am sure of it."

Dad happily told Leroy that he was terribly sorry they "wouldn't be spending time together today," and wished him well in the future. Leroy left, confused, and I was left with my mother and father in awkward silence.

Knowing such things should be discussed thoroughly, I asked my father if he was afraid of dying.

He smiled again, but this time as if with his whole body, he exclaimed: "Not at all! I am looking forward to my GREAT ADVENTURE!"

Reflecting on that surprising burst of energy, I blurted out: "Well, Dad, the good news is now you can eat anything you want. What's your heart's desire right now?"

"Oh, son," he brightened up even more. "I have been craving a McDonald's chocolate milkshake."

"Gotta go, Mom," I said, and we quickly raced out to bring back an extra-large McDonald's chocolate shake.

The three of us sat there quietly, as Dad sucked heavily on the thick, sweet milkshake.

I realized that what I loved him for was not the fame but the *courage* to make his decision to stop dialysis, the *commitment* he had made to care for his wife until he needed total care himself, and the *honor* with which he handled my demented mother's most-embarrassing moments.

No longer the tall, imposing figure in a Navy-blue uniform with gold stars covering each shoulder, my father sat unsteadily on his hospital bed with his backside exposed under loose ties in the hospital gown that his tremulous hands could no longer handle.

Wordlessly, he kept sucking down that thick chocolate shake as if his life depended on it.

When he finished, being careful not to slurp the last bit, he looked up at me with a lock of oily hair tangling with his bushy eyebrows.

"Son," he said, "life is so gooooood!"

A few days later, Vice Admiral Marmaduke Gresham Bayne III died in his sleep, fully at peace with this world, and excited about the next.

CHAPTER 37

Chasing the dream

"Where do we get such passions in life, anyway?

AFTER A HALF-CENTURY OF PRACTICING MEDICINE, most of which has been dominated by my insane drive to bring back physician house calls, I find myself wondering how this career became such an obsession.

And where, in fact, do we get such passions in life, anyway?

What separates those of us who dare to take the risk of starting a new enterprise, chasing that dream beyond all reason?

Spending $30 million of other people's money over 30 years with negligible profit is certainly nothing to be proud of, but it all depends upon your definition of success.

My primary goal was never to become wealthy, but rather to begin a return to the fundamentals of medicine by a focus on home-based treatment for the most potentially costly patients.

~◆◆◆~

In that, we have undeniably begun a movement.

Today, there are house call programs in every major city in the U.S.

Moreover, the Centers for Medicare and Medicaid, a federal agency within the U.S. Department of Health and Human Services (HHS), in 2019 launched a five-year Independence at Home program.

The goal was to save large amounts of taxpayers' dollars through the delivery of physician house calls, all the while providing fair and just compensation for health-care providers and reducing overall costs.

House call payments have tripled since I started making them full-time in 1985, making it a financially-feasible medical career. Numerous articles have been published establishing the cost-effectiveness and beneficial outcomes of home-based care in the most critical and complex of patients.

Most of all, the trend is driven by what many patients want in the first place: Quality home-based medical care, available to all.

For some 30 years now, along with a small group of fellow evangelicals at the Academy of Home Care Medicine, I have been expecting our minor "house call movement" to become more and more mainstream.

Hasn't happened as yet, but there are promising signs of house calls becoming more of a respected site of practice for up-and-coming physicians.

Despite the success of our programs, years of proven cost-effective research, better patient outcomes in virtually every study done, and universal appeal to those who practice mobile medicine full-time, the hidden forces of a $3.7 trillion healthcare industry continue to resist.

Though resistance remains, I'm gratified that some measurable progress has been made.

—◦◦◦—

I have often wondered how much of my own stubborn resistance – borne of the passion I still feel for my mission to help others through medicine – came from my father.

On those rare occasions when he was home, I remember him telling me words I've never forgotten: "Find something you are passionate about, and then become an expert in it."

That became my own life's story.

Deciding to start and operate Call Doctor was literally the only professional pursuit since graduating from medical school that I did for more than three years. I'm forever grateful that I made such a commitment.

Certainly, I've been privileged to follow some very big shoes, and perhaps lucky to be afflicted with a huge dose of inherited ADHD that only became sublimated when I started making house calls.

Looking back, I never would've found my way without discovering the intimacy of providing care and comfort in my patients' homes, and the timeless lessons they taught me about my profession, their lives and my own life journey.

I have been lucky in so many ways.

CHAPTER 38

Blissfully unaware

"It just wouldn't be right."

THE HOUSE CALL I MADE IN EARLY 2001 in Williamsburg, Virginia while visiting my parents was unexpected.

At least partly, I was there to attend a luncheon with "our dear friend, who has lost his wife of 62 years." Mom and Dad had retired to nearby Irvington, Virginia and made friends with nearly everybody as far as I could tell.

By then, my mother was an accomplished artist and taught art to the residents of Westminster-Canterbury, the old-age home where my father was to die, and where she was herself to exist, blissfully unaware of her surroundings, for the last decades of her life.

Dad, of course, stayed busy commuting to Washington, D.C., where he had been appointed the Councilor to the School of Arab Studies at Georgetown University.

That meant he originated the Bahraini-American Friendship Society (notice the order of the names) and raised some $25 million so students at Georgetown could learn about the complex issues facing the Middle East.

Along the way, my father turned down an offer from his dear friend, Shaikh Isa bin Sulman al Khalifah, the Emir of Bahrain. The Bahraini government wanted to pay him a commission of $250,000 per boat for at least ten littoral attack vessels they intended to buy from the U.S. to patrol their coastal waters.

I remember asking my father why he didn't take the lucrative kickback, which was legal at that time, from his Arabian friends.

"It just wouldn't be right," was all he said.

The luncheon was hosted by the kind of man who always seemed to be hanging around my father. His home was gorgeous, seemingly a replica of Monticello, but located on the waters of Carter's Creek, a lovely hurricane hole off the mouth of the Rappahannock River in southern Virginia.

Out of nowhere, our host casually informed us that he was one of the early investors in what is now called a unicorn, the kind of stock investment which returns millions for each dollar you dared to risk in the beginning.

The table looked like one of the official state dinners my parents used to attend at the various governors' home of former English territories in any number of East Africa countries.

Obviously wealthy beyond description, our host felt the need to explain he didn't deserve it.

At the end of the seemingly pointless luncheon, the frail, 80-ish man I would describe as "dapper," pulled me aside and said: "I know you are creating a house call network around the nation, but here in rural Virginia, we won't get a mobile physician for years. Will you help me stockpile the right drugs, so when the time comes, I can exit this earth on my own terms?"

There it was.

The most complicated question physicians face today in the privacy of people's homes relegated to a "by the way" on my way out the door. I was completely flummoxed, which is to say I had no coherent thought as to how to continue the conversation on his doorstep.

—⁓—

Finally, I blurted something like: "This is a much more complex question than we should engage in at this moment. Perhaps I may contact you later, after I am back in San Diego and we can discuss with you the risks and benefits of such a plan?"

He made me promise to call, one of the many promises I failed to keep throughout my professional life. The guilt still pervades my soul.

Moreover, it is a topic that must be addressed by every mobile clinician who sees sick patients in their home.

For centuries, doctors had been honored with questions like this for the trust they had earned, for the counsel they gave "their" patients at the final hour.

I never thought physician-assisted suicide was an option in my practice, yet California law now makes it legal. To me, the decision to treat a dying patient by relieving their suffering, even when such medications may abbreviate their life unexpectedly, is one of the sacrosanct privileges that comes with being a physician.

My medical career now seems discordant with the transition from traditional values to a more modern, "managed-care friendly" approach.

From Dr. Kevorkian's death stories to criminal prosecution of well-meaning physicians performing acts which today would be considered compassionate, the application of man-made laws has failed to solve the seminal question we all have at the end of life: "What is the appropriate role for a physician when the patient actively seeks passage to the afterlife?"

I think Hippocrates had it right:

"I will respect the privacy of my patients, for their problems are not disclosed to me that the world may know. Most especially must I tread with care in matters of life and death. If it is given me to save a life, all thanks.

"But it may also be within my power to take a life; this awesome responsibility must be faced with great humbleness and awareness of my own frailty. Above all, I must not play at God."

—◆—

I graduated from the Medical College of Virginia (MCV) in 1973. Since 1838, MCV had been educating doctors using the Hippocratic Oath as a final, testamentary standard.

Our Class of 1973 was the last class required to take the Hippocratic Oath in the school's history. It was a mistake to have stopped the practice.

———✺———

Over the years, I learned a great deal about the Navy's core values of *honor, commitment* and *courage* from my father and the men and women with whom he associated.

For one thing, I learned that it takes courage to leave a lucrative academic position to start a heretical mobile medical practice. Being on the front page of The Wall Street Journal might sound exciting, but the headline of "Winnebago Doc" left something to be desired.

I learned that one must honor the patient's wishes above all else … above their ability to pay, above any concerns about the community standard of care, above any criticism by more traditional doctors in their office-based practices, above one's own perceptions as to what level of aggressive care seems appropriate.

I learned it takes commitment … to raise $30 million in nine rounds of venture capital funding; to change the payment rules for Medicare home visits; to write a law, get it through Congress and signed by the President proving the clinical and societal (fiscal) advantages of house calls for a particular subset of highly-complex, high-cost patients.

Most of all, I learned that the majority of our very-sick patients demonstrated their own version of honor, courage and commitment.

From the family of a U.S. Army Surgeon General left brain-dead by his heart attack while teaching Sunday School, I learned that there is honor in a dignified death, even if I had to break state law to arrange it.

I learned courage from the quadriplegic with multiple sclerosis whom I often visited more for my own cheering up than any real need of hers … until the day she complained of weakness, and I had to tell her she had also developed a fatal form of leukemia.

Smiling genuinely as she refused further treatment, she quietly informed me that "God has given me these past 16 years motionless in bed to make my peace with Him. It is enough."

From the man who sank the largest warship ever built, I learned how one can face imminent death and still use your last breath to compliment the efforts of your house call doctor; how a commitment to be there when he needs you can wreck family vacations, but sometimes save a life worth saving.

Having begun this journey full of egoism and wanting credit for bringing back the house call, I end it with nothing but admiration for that courageous group of patients who allowed me to care for their catastrophic needs. They have introduced me to a type of love that is called "agape."

It is a type of love for one's fellow man and respect for their suffering that requires personal sacrifice. It is a love that grows out of intimacy.

I had no idea the mere fact I made house calls when people were truly in need would lead to such rich and enduring relationships. This intense bonding enabled a greater personal commitment and made it easier to alter my own lifestyle to enjoy the richness of such mutual trust.

I began feeling called on to apply my advanced clinical skills, enabled by new technologies, to replace the inane healthcare systems that have evolved from America's current disjointed payment system. Selfishly, I looked forward to becoming famous, possibly even wealthy as an entrepreneur.

Now, after making more than 10,000 house calls, I'm able to reflect on my career with a deeper understanding of my value. I have learned that the power of home visits lies not in its opportunity to save Medicare and balance the budget, but in its ability to restore the doctor-patient relationship.

It is such relationships that drive all progress, and the most powerful of all of these is caring deeply for the health and well-being of your fellow man and woman.

"Life is so gooood..."

When?

I entered quietly, trying not to see
where I found her, amidst the odors
that were never meant to be.

An old man sits confused
by the chair I refuse
for reasons known only to me.
How could I shame them?

Bent, gracious, solicitous to a fault
he heaps praise on me,
expecting miracles.
I bob and weave, a doctor's trick.

She is dying soon, I fear,
but do they know?
Is this their apogee,
Or a blow that ends his 86 years?

Trapped again in my house call,
evolving tragedy with pictures on the wall.
Why not share the glories of the War they won,
the sons they raised, remember their fun?

This time the cardiologist was right.
A chest over-filled with heart
belies her day, warns of coming night.
Her fight is almost over.

He offers me tea.
I tell him she will die soon.

He thanks me for the comfort I've brought.
I feel stupid saying how hard she fought.

Oh, how I loathe this practice I love so much,
The mistakes I've made, the lives I've touched.
How much easier to fix a spleen,
repair a wound, ignore the screams
where lights are bright, and it smells so clean?

Unequal to the task, I feel despair.
Here, in their home, there's no place to hide.
His heart, too, is broken, beyond repair.
Where people die, it's harder to lie.

He softly asks me again: "But when?"

C. Gresham Bayne, M.D.